S. HRG. 113–457

LEBANON AT THE CROSSROADS

HEARING

BEFORE THE

SUBCOMMITTEE ON NEAR EASTERN AND
SOUTH AND CENTRAL ASIAN AFFAIRS

OF THE

COMMITTEE ON FOREIGN RELATIONS
UNITED STATES SENATE

ONE HUNDRED THIRTEENTH CONGRESS

SECOND SESSION

FEBRUARY 25, 2014

Printed for the use of the Committee on Foreign Relations

Available via the World Wide Web: http://www.gpo.gov/fdsys/

U.S. GOVERNMENT PRINTING OFFICE

91–137 PDF   WASHINGTON : 2014

For sale by the Superintendent of Documents, U.S. Government Printing Office
Internet: bookstore.gpo.gov   Phone: toll free (866) 512–1800; DC area (202) 512–1800
Fax: (202) 512–2104   Mail: Stop IDCC, Washington, DC 20402–0001

(II)

CONTENTS

LEBANON AT THE CROSSROADS

TUESDAY, FEBRUARY 25, 2014

U.S. SENATE,
SUBCOMMITTEE ON NEAR EASTERN AND
SOUTH AND CENTRAL ASIAN AFFAIRS,
COMMITTEE ON FOREIGN RELATIONS,
Washington, DC.

The subcommittee met, pursuant to notice, at 3:44 p.m., in room SD–419, Dirksen Senate Office Building, Hon. Tim Kaine (chairman of the subcommittee) presiding.

Present: Senators Kaine and Risch.

OPENING STATEMENT OF HON. TIM KAINE, U.S. SENATOR FROM VIRGINIA

Senator KAINE. I want to call this meeting of the Senate Foreign Relations Committee, the Subcommittee on the Near Eastern, South and Central Asian Affairs to order.

I want to welcome all who are here, especially our four expert witnesses who we will hear testimony from today.

The Senate is currently in the middle of a vote on a veterans bill that will take a bit of time, but I want to take advantage of folks being here. We will proceed to a first panel and then a second panel with questions. And this is a very important topic.

The topic of the hearing today is "Lebanon at the Crossroads." I just returned from a trip in Lebanon last week with Senator Angus King of Maine. We went together because we serve together on the Armed Services and Budget Committees, but we also serve separately. I am on the Foreign Relations Committee, obviously, and Senator King is on the Intelligence Committee. We took a trip where we spent time in Israel, Palestine, Lebanon, and Egypt. In some ways, I think we were probably most excited about the trip to Lebanon because neither of us had been to Lebanon. We have strong feelings about the situation there, but we felt like we needed to ground those feelings and thoughts with some reality check.

On the basis of that trip, I do feel very strongly that the title of this hearing is apt. Lebanon is at a crossroads. The Syrian conflict, about which we spent so much time in Foreign Relations and Armed Services, has devastated Syria and many of its neighbors, but I think at least in the American press and in the telling of the story about Syrian effects, Lebanon is often an overlooked neighbor with respect to stories about the Syrian crisis.

Lebanon has been extremely generous in welcoming Syrian refugees into the country, as has been its tradition. And it has paid the highest price, I believe, in terms of the stability and security of the country. Lebanon deserves our attention and continued investment and partnership, and if we do that and we do it the right way, it will be good for the country and good for regional and global security.

In July 2013, Senator King and I, in separate congressional trips, visited Turkey and Jordan, and when we were in Turkey and Jordan, we saw, experienced, visited refugee camps and talked with leaders about the strain of Syrian refugees on those U.S. partners. But it was important that we go back to Lebanon to have those same discussions, and what we saw was challenging. The population of Lebanon is a little bit over 4 million and there is nearly a million—by many accounts, more than a million—Syrian refugees in Lebanon from Syria on top of refugees who have already been there from Palestine for many decades.

Kind of wrapping your head around the notion of a refugee population that has come in the last couple years equivalent to 25 percent of the population of the country is pretty dramatic. Imagine 80 million war refugees coming to the United States over the period of about 2 years. That would be 25 percent of our population. You can imagine how many challenges that would pose. And that size of refugee population obviously poses many, many significant difficulties for Lebanese civil society.

Senator King and I set up this CODEL to visit Lebanon a couple of months ago, but through the fortuity of timing, right before we arrived in the country, the Government of Lebanon was able to form after many months of gridlock. As many of you know who follow Lebanon, the challenge of forming a government among competing factions with Cabinet ministries in a sufficient ratio to receive parliamentary approval is very, very difficult. We had a chance to be the first congressional delegation to meet with Prime Minister Salam and with President Suleiman after the formation of this government. We offered congratulations on the formation of the government, and we discussed with each of them the relatively prompt path for Presidential elections and the need to keep that path on time and the need for a balanced and strong ministerial statement, that statement of government that is done within 30 days of the formation of the government that establishes key priorities for this government in this phase.

We think the formation of the government with Presidential elections in Lebanon—and the President is elected by Parliament on a two-thirds vote—the carrying out of Presidential elections with parliamentary elections to follow should provide assistance and should help in administering some of the challenges that result from the Syrian refugees. But that will not be at all sufficient. There must be much more work done by international partners, including the United States, if we care about the stability of Lebanon.

During our time there, we met not only with elected officials. We also met with many NGOs administering aid to Syrian refugees. We met with members of Parliament and Cabinet ministers in the newly formed government. We met with the UNHCR Administrator, Ninette Kelley, to talk about refugee issues. And what we found bluntly was again and again even if we would ask questions about Lebanese internal issues, within a very short time the answer would end up being about Syria and about the Syrian challenge, not only the refugees coming into the country, but how the decision of the Hezbollah organization to participate so actively and visibly in the Syrian civil war has increased violence, largely Sunni-Shia violence, within the country of Lebanon.

It was a challenging trip. One morning we were leaving the American Embassy to go have a meeting with President Suleiman and a bomb went off in downtown Beirut near where we were. You could hear it. You could see the smoke. This was an everyday event to many, sadly. We assumed that our meeting with President Suleiman would be canceled. If it were here, a bomb going off—two motorcycles exploding a bomb that killed many and injured many, many more in a part of downtown near where a meeting—the President would say, I got my hands full, I do not want to have the meeting. But President Suleiman basically wanted us to see the kind of challenge that he was dealing with. And so the meeting continued and in the midst of the meeting, the President was being interrupted with phone calls to try to talk to the Iranian Ambassador. This particular bombing was near an Iranian cultural center to talk to others.

And it was a little bit heartbreaking to see the normality of the situation and to feel as visitors—we were just there for a brief time—but the challenge that must pose for the everyday life of those who might be caught in the cross-fire of violence occurring in random ways in random neighborhoods.

On the question of Syria, I think we all agree that U.S. diplomatic energies notwithstanding, we are not happy with the path that the situation in Syria is taking, not by a long shot. The United States is the largest provider of humanitarian aid to Syrian refugees outside the country, including in Lebanon. The aid we give is through the U.N. and then distributed through worthy NGOs. We are the largest provider of humanitarian aid. We are deeply engaged in negotiations around the eventual destruction of the chemical weapons stockpile in Syria. We are deeply engaged in efforts at the U.N. Security Council or in Geneva to try to find the path forward. But while we are deeply engaged, we are not happy with the process and the progress. And so that continues to pose challenges that could be of a longstanding nature for Lebanon.

Weeks ago, I called for a resolution, after meeting with victims of civil war in Syria who exited Syria through Lebanon, to try to provide more aggressive insertion of humanitarian aid into Syria, not just the provision of aid to Syrian refugees outside the country, but to focus on aid inside Syria. The U.N. last week adopted a resolution, finally overcoming Russia's propensity to veto, along with the support of China, even humanitarian aid resolutions. Last week there was a little bit of a breakthrough on that. But frankly, whether it was a breakthrough or not will only be determined by whether humanitarian aid starts to be delivered in a more significant way.

But if we are to try to tackle the challenges and be a good partner and ally in Lebanon, we need to continue that, the delivery of humanitarian aid in Syria, the provision of humanitarian aid for refugees who have exited Syria, and a continued effort diplomatically to try to find a path to a resolution or cease-fire in the civil war.

During our visit to Lebanon, we also had the opportunity to visit with Lebanese Armed Forces and explore the ways in which the United States is working in tandem with the armed forces. We found a high degree of satisfaction with that relationship within the armed forces. Many of the armed forces leaders we met in the Lebanese Armed Forces had done training either in the United States or with U.S. military leaders. And I would say throughout the region, probably in Lebanon the degree of satisfaction in the mil-to-mil relationship was probably the highest.

That military armed forces has a significant challenge because in some critical areas, the armed forces are weaker than the Hezbollah militia. That is an unusual situation to contemplate from an American standpoint where it would not be imaginable that a militia in the United States would be more powerful than the armed forces. It kind of challenges concepts that you have about the strength of armed forces. But every day and in numerous ways, the American military leadership is working with the Lebanese Armed Forces to increase capacity, whether it is technology or training, and we found a high degree of satisfaction and appreciation for those relationships. We want to make sure that we continue this because it is not just the Syrian effect, but it is also al-Qaeda and other extremist groups that we worry about. They must not be able to establish a base of operations in Lebanon.

We want to ensure that United States policy and support for Lebanon remain strong, and we feel like the plight in Lebanon is an untold story of the Syrian civil war.

Finally, before I introduce our first panel and we ask them to make opening statements and have a bit of a dialogue, the other reason to have this is our Lebanese American population is such a strong part of America. One of the reasons you do hearings like this is not only to cast a spotlight on a part of the world where a story has not been told, but also to honor Americans whose tradition and heritage is such that they have strong connections in Lebanon. And Lebanese Americans are often not removed from Lebanon. They are deeply engaged in Lebanon. We find that in Virginia and in so many communities throughout the United States. The Lebanese American contribution to our society, whether it is the foundation of St. Jude's Hospital which is a spectacular story or so many other areas, is something that is really notable. And when we have significant chunks of our population who care so deeply about their own homes, that in and of itself is a reason for the United States to be focused as well.

So both because of the critical role of Lebanon in the Middle East but also because of this strong Lebanese American population in this country we decided to hold this hearing and focus on ways where the United States can continue to be a partner but find strategies and ways to be better partners.

We have two panels with us.

Senator Risch is the ranking member on the Subcommittee on the Near East, South and Central Asia, and I suspect Senator Risch will be here when the vote on the veterans bill is done at some point. When he arrives, I will ask if he has opening comments, and I may interrupt the testimony.

But I want to move in to our two panels. Our first panel is two distinguished folks. I will introduce them both and then ask each to give opening statements. Then we will get into a dialogue.

Larry Silverman is Acting Deputy Assistant Secretary of State for Near Eastern Affairs. Mr. Silverman was helpful in prepping me and Senator King to go do the visit to Lebanon last week. He has been Director of Israel and Palestinian Affairs for the Department of State and also served as Vice President Biden's Special Advisor for Europe and Russia. During the first half of his career, Mr. Silverman focused on issues related to the Middle East, serving overseas in Jordan and Syria and in Washington, served as special advisor to Bill Burns. Mr. Silverman, glad to have you with us.

We are also pleased to be joined today by Maj. Gen. Mike Plehn, who is the Principal Director for Middle East Policy in the Office of the Secretary of Defense for policy. General Plehn helps execute defense policy and national security strategy for 15 Middle East nations, including Lebanon. And we are happy to have him with us today.

With those introductions, I would like to ask Mr. Silverman first to offer your testimony. We accept your written testimony into the record. Try to summarize within 5 minutes. Then General Plehn. Then we will get into question and answer.

STATEMENT OF LAWRENCE SILVERMAN, ACTING DEPUTY ASSISTANT SECRETARY FOR NEAR EASTERN AFFAIRS, U.S. DEPARTMENT OF STATE, WASHINGTON, DC

Mr. SILVERMAN. Thank you very much, Mr. Chairman Kaine, and thank you for inviting me today to testify on the situation in Lebanon and our policy toward that very important country in a very volatile region as you saw directly.

Your hearing comes at an important moment for Lebanon's security and stability. Public discussion of Lebanon, as you say, in the United States has often focused primarily on the impact of the Syrian refugee flows into that country. The refugee crisis that you witnessed firsthand during your recent visit to Lebanon represents an urgent, imperative need.

That said, Lebanon faces broader issues, and the United States is helping Lebanon respond to these challenges because Lebanon's future affects important U.S. interests in the region, which are very obvious just by the geographical nature of Lebanon's location and its neighborhood.

The Syrian conflict threatens progress and Lebanon's attempt to cement national identity and to establish lasting stability and an effective political system. The February 15 formation of a government by Prime Minister Salam, after 10 months of gridlock, is a welcome development for the Lebanese people and an opportunity for the United States and Lebanon to work together to achieve shared goals.

The Lebanese people deserve a government that responds to their needs and protects their interests. As it works to gain a vote of confidence from Parliament and begins to exercise full powers, this government is in one sense better than its predecessor. Nearly all political factions are represented in a careful balance. The March 14 faction is in the government.

In order to obtain confidence, the Cabinet, as you say, must now agree on a ministerial policy statement. We have expressed support for this government. How we work with it will depend on its policies and its actions.

The next political hurdle, as you know, is the end of President Suleiman's term in office on May 25. Presidential elections should be conducted on time, freely, and fairly, and without foreign interference. We hope that the spirit that led to the government formation will also ensure that there is no Presidential vacancy.

I think you know already, Mr. Chairman, of Lebanon's unique security problems: a porous border, Hezbollah's weapon stockpiles beyond government control, the need for all armed groups to be disarmed. And you know that existing political and sectarian differences have been intensified by the war in Syria. Hezbollah entered that war contrary to the agreement of all Lebanese parties to dissociate Lebanon from foreign conflicts. Hezbollah, on behalf of its foreign supporters, is dragging the Lebanese people into a war in defense of the Assad regime. Hezbollah's posture of acting inside the state when it is convenient but stepping outside the state to use arms and violence when it wishes is deeply threatening. And now extremists fighting the Assad regime and its Hezbollah backers have brought their fight inside Lebanon, through a wave of reprehensible terrorist attacks that have killed and injured scores in Beirut and other cities.

Amidst this, the Lebanese Armed Forces have acted to maintain internal security. Just 3 days ago, two Lebanese Armed Forces soldiers were killed in a terrorist suicide bombing. As you know, the LAF has had recent counterterrorism successes, capturing some high-profile terrorists, including a facilitator for al-Qaeda-affiliated groups responsible for several suicide bombings.

These incidents highlight the ongoing dangers from Hezbollah's support for the Assad regime and the flow of violent extremists, whether they be from the al-Nusra Front version in Lebanon, the Islamic State of Iraq, and the Levant, and the Abdullah Azzam Brigades, the last of which claim responsibilities for the most recent bombings.

The critical material and training we provide to the LAF and the internal security forces builds their capacities to conduct operations against extremists, terrorists, and criminal organizations. My colleague, General Plehn, will offer details on this. We are trying to increase our foreign military financing to the LAF in order to modernize it and build its capabilities, particularly to secure its border with Syria.

Mr. Chairman, we need to maintain the strong partnership we have built with the LAF. And we appreciate Congress for its continued support of State and Defense programs that enhance Lebanon's security and economic development.

Mr. Chairman, you saw and you said that Lebanon hosts more Syrian refugees than any other country in the region, nearly 940,000 or more. There is not a single Lebanese community that has not been affected by the refugee crisis. The United States is doing its part to help Lebanon deal with the burden, providing over

$340 million in assistance. We urge other countries to meet the pledges that they have made.

There has also been a very damaging economic spillover to the tourism sector to investment and trade. The World Bank has estimated that the crisis will cut real GDP growth by 2.9 percent this year, and losses from the conflict would reach $7.5 billion.

The most promising economic sector would be possible substantial reserves of offshore natural gas and even oil deposits. We hope those will be explored and contracted, and the State Department is engaging with both Lebanon and Israel to see about potential solutions to their maritime boundary dispute.

Secretary General of the United Nations, Ban Ki-moon, and President Suleiman last September launched the International Support Group for Lebanon. We look to this group not to be a one-off in September, but to be an active vehicle by which the international community can provide the support to promote stability. Secretary Kerry will attend the next gathering of this group, the International Support Group, in Paris next week.

The United States is also committed to ensuring an end to the era of impunity and assassinations and political violence in Lebanon. That is why we strongly support the work of the Special Tribunal for Lebanon, which just began 1 month ago the trials to determine and bring to justice those responsible for assassinating former Prime Minister, Rafik Hariri, and dozens of others. The Lebanese people, Mr. Chairman, have waited too long for accountability and justice. Unfortunately, as we all know, political violence still plagues Lebanon. Just in December, former Finance Minister and Ambassador to the United States, Mohammad Chatah, was assassinated.

Mr. Chairman, Lebanon has faced existential challenges since its independence. The Taif Accord in 1989 helped end the civil war. U.N. Security Council Resolutions 1559 and 1701 helped structure a return to stability, and the 2012 Baabda Declaration established the principle that all Lebanese parties and factions should abstain from regional conflicts. It needs to be implemented. The Baabda Declaration needs to be implemented by all parties.

Fortunately, amidst all these problems, Lebanon also has friends, and the United States counts itself as a very important friend of Lebanon and will continue to be. We need to stand with the people of Lebanon now. It is in our national interest to promote a stable Lebanon, free of foreign interference and able to defend its interests.

Thank you and I look forward to your questions.

[The prepared statement of Mr. Silverman follows:]

PREPARED STATEMENT OF LAWRENCE SILVERMAN

Chairman Kaine, Ranking Member Risch, members of the subcommittee, thank you for inviting me to testify today on the situation in Lebanon and our policy toward that important country in a very volatile region.

Your hearing comes at an important moment for Lebanon's security and stability—and that of the entire Levant. Public discussion of Lebanon in the United States has often focused primarily on the impact of the Syrian refugee flows into the country. This attention, including the Senate's hearing on this subject last December, is warranted.

Mr. Chairman, the refugee crisis that you witnessed first-hand during your recent visit to Lebanon represents an urgent, imperative need. That said, it is one of several issues Lebanon's leaders and the Lebanese people face today. In addition to the refugee crisis, I would like to discuss today the political, security and economic challenges Lebanon faces, and how the United States is responding to all these challenges, because Lebanon's future affects important U.S. interests in the region.

The United States has a long history of diplomatic engagement with Lebanon to promote our interests in regional stability, the development of democracy, economic prosperity, and the effort to counter terrorism and extremism. We have worked to support and rebuild Lebanese state institutions that were left in ruins as a result of the civil war, and we have provided development assistance that helps to improve the lives and livelihoods of Lebanese citizens. Since the end of the Syrian occupation in 2005, we have accelerated our assistance to crucial state institutions to enable them to take on the leadership roles and management functions that a national government should perform.

Mr. Chairman, it is essential that the international community stand by responsible forces in Lebanon in a broader sense, and particularly so in the next several months. Let me explain why.

POLITICAL CHALLENGES

Lebanon is at a critical point in its attempt to cement a national identity and to establish lasting stability and an effective political system. The conflict in Syria threatens the progress it has made. Lebanon's political leaders face a series of political hurdles in the first few months of this year; it has just overcome the first of these. The February 15 formation of a government by Prime Minister Salam, after 10 months of stalemate and gridlock, is a welcome development for the Lebanese people and an opportunity for the United States and Lebanon to work together toward shared goals. We thank former Prime Minister Najib Mikati for his service, and we thank President Michel Sleiman, who has worked to steer Lebanon during very difficult times, and who worked with PM-designate Salam for months to form this Cabinet.

The Lebanese people deserve a government that responds to their needs and protects their interests. This new government is comprised of eight members from the March 14 coalition, eight from the March 8 coalition, and eight others without formal affiliation. As it works to gain a vote of confidence from Parliament and begins to exercise its full powers, this new government is in a sense an improvement over its predecessor: nearly all political factions are represented in a careful balance, and after 3 years outside of government, the March 14 coalition is now part of the Cabinet.

It is clear that the March 14 coalition determined that its interests in stabilizing Lebanon and promoting democracy and good governance were better served by participating in this government. In order to gain that vote of confidence, the Cabinet must first come to agreement on a ministerial policy statement. We have expressed support for the new government, but how we will work with it depends on its policies and actions.

The next political hurdle facing Lebanon is the end of President Sleiman's term in office on May 25. We have made clear to all those concerned in Lebanon that the United States believes Presidential elections should be conducted on time, freely and fairly, and without foreign interference. We hope that the interest in a stable Lebanon that drove the parties to reach agreement on the new Cabinet will also drive them to ensure that there is no vacancy. Lebanon needs responsible leadership that will address the challenges facing Lebanon and fulfill Lebanon's international obligations.

SECURITY CHALLENGES

Lebanon has truly unique security problems: an undemarcated and porous border with Syria that facilitates terrorist infiltration; areas of the country outside full state control; Hezbollah's weapon stockpiles beyond government authority; the continuing need to implement UNSCR 1701 that called for the disarmament of all armed groups in Lebanon and stressed the importance of full control of Lebanon by the Government of Lebanon; and a history of foreign interference in its internal matters.

Mr. Chairman, as you saw clearly during your visit, challenges to Lebanon's security are rising. Existing political and sectarian differences have been intensified by the war in Syria. Hezbollah entered that war against the earlier agreement of all Lebanese parties and the Lebanese Government to "dissociate" the country from foreign conflicts. The Lebanese people know only too well the repercussions of spillover from the Assad regime's brutal suppression of its own people. Syrian aircraft and artillery have violated Lebanon's borders with impunity. Hezbollah is dragging the

Lebanese people into a war in defense of an Assad regime whose continuation can only result in more conflict, more terrorism, and more instability for Lebanon. It does so not in the interest of Lebanon, but in its own narrow interests and on behalf of its foreign sponsors. Hezbollah's posture of acting inside the state when it is convenient, but stepping outside the state to use arms and violence when it deems necessary for its self-interests remains deeply disturbing and threatening.

And now, extremists fighting the Assad regime and its Hezbollah backers have brought that fight inside Lebanon, through a wave of reprehensible terrorist attacks that have killed and injured scores in Beirut and other cities.

The Lebanese Armed Forces (LAF) has acted to maintain internal security, and it has taken losses in those operations. Twenty LAF soldiers were killed in a June 2013 attempt to arrest an extremist and his followers in Sidon, and the LAF has intervened a number of times in Tripoli in an effort to mitigate politico-sectarian clashes. The LAF has had some recent counterterrorism successes. It has captured a number of high-profile terrorists, including a facilitator for several al-Qaeda-affiliated groups that have carried out a spate of brutal suicide bombings in Beirut, Hermel, and other Lebanese towns.

Mr. Chairman, as our Ambassador in Beirut, David Hale, said of the terrorist incident that occurred during your visit, ''these abhorrent acts of . . . terrorism threaten the principles of stability, freedom, and safety that the people of Lebanon have worked so hard to uphold and we urge all parties to refrain from retaliatory acts that contribute to the cycle of violence.''

These incidents highlight the ongoing dangers to Lebanon from the Syrian conflict, Hezbollah's armed support for the Assad regime, and the flow of violent extremists (such as the Nusra Front, the Islamic State of Iraq, and the Levant, and the Abdullah Azzam Brigades) into Lebanon, who seek to justify their indiscriminate attacks as retaliation against Hezbollah's involvement in Syria. Of course, the flow of these fighters is a problem for several states in the region. The states from which these fighters are coming are concerned about the dangers these fighters will present when they return to their home countries.

Central to any country's stability is a trained and capable security sector that is accountable to the people and the state. The critical support we provide to the LAF and the Internal Security Forces (ISF) is intended to build their capacities to conduct operations against extremists and criminal organizations and to ensure security throughout the country, including along its borders. Our assistance to the LAF—the United States has provided over 70 percent of LAF acquisitions—strengthens its ability to serve as the sole institution entrusted with the defense of Lebanon's sovereignty.

We are trying to increase this assistance in order to modernize the LAF, and in particular to build its capabilities to secure its own borders with Syria, which are porous. Providing the LAF with the ability to better control its borders is crucial.

U.S. assistance helps ensure that extremist actors, such as Hezbollah, Iran, or the Syrian regime, have minimal opportunity to influence the LAF. We continually assess our policy of engagement with and assistance to the Government of Lebanon to ensure that no foreign terrorist organizations (including but not limited to Hezbollah) influence or benefit from the assistance we provide to the LAF and the ISF.

Our sustained support through the funding that Congress approves—FMF, IMET, and DOD 1206 funds—is critical to improving the capabilities of the LAF. Our IMET program in particular has built lasting professional relationships between the senior ranks of the LAF and the U.S. military, as well as strengthened the values of civilian leadership and respect for rule of law within the LAF officer corps. My Department of Defense colleague, General Plehn, will provide greater detail of our relationship with the LAF, but I want to emphasize the importance of the relationships we have built with the LAF and with the ISF over the years. My DOD colleagues and we thank you for your continued support of State and Defense programs that provide for Lebanon's security and economic development.

As Chairman Kaine heard directly from LAF Commander Kahwagi in Lebanon, the LAF is a beacon of cross-confessional integration for the entire country. It remains one of the most respected national institutions in Lebanon because it reflects the diversity of the country: it is in fact the sole national institution able to counter destabilizing influences from within Lebanon and without. Supporting the LAF strengthens its ability to serve as a model for other Lebanese institutions. Our assistance has been effective and is welcomed by Lebanon; it has helped create important relationships. We need to maintain this strong partnership.

You have seen reports that Saudi Arabia will provide $3 billion for the LAF. International assistance to the LAF can help build up the capabilities the LAF needs. The United States believes international donors can complement each other's efforts in order to maximize the growth of needed capabilities for an armed force whose troops are badly stretched across the country. We are in contact with the Governments of Saudi Arabia and France regarding this assistance to promote maximum coordination.

Lebanon hosts more Syrian refugees than any other country—both per capita and in absolute terms. There are currently nearly 940,000 Syrian refugees—some 20 percent of the total population now, as well as 51,000 Palestinian refugees from Syria in Lebanon, of which the vast majority reside in host communities in rented accommodations, unfinished buildings, or in informal tented settlements in more than 1,600 localities throughout the country. There is not a single Lebanese community that has not been affected by the refugee crisis. With refugee arrivals continuing, the sheer volume of need has overwhelmed ability of the central government and local municipalities to respond to the enormous challenge of providing public services to this large and growing population.

The United States is doing its part, providing over $340 million in humanitarian assistance since the beginning of the Syrian conflict to support the needs of refugees in Lebanon and the communities that host them, including $76.4 million announced by Secretary Kerry at the International Humanitarian Pledging Conference for Syria held in Kuwait a month ago. Last September at the inaugural meeting of the International Support Group for Lebanon, Secretary Kerry announced $30 million in assistance specifically aimed at helping the communities that host these refugees. As you know, Lebanon does not have formal refugee camps for Syrians; almost all of the refugees from Syria live in Lebanese communities, placing strains on basic infrastructure and health and educational systems. We appreciate the generosity and hospitality of the Lebanese Government and the Lebanese people and understand the enormity of the influx.

In its most recent humanitarian appeal, the U.N. is seeking $1.7 billion in 2014 to adequately respond to the refugee crisis in Lebanon, on top of the money that the government of Lebanon is already spending on the crisis. The scope of the crisis is an unprecedented challenge for the U.N. humanitarian agencies and nongovernmental organizations; the Lebanese will face this challenge for some time. The international community must step up to provide both humanitarian and development assistance to assist these refugees and the communities that host them in order to bolster Lebanon's stability while meeting urgent humanitarian needs.

We urge those countries that have made pledges of funds for Lebanon and the other neighboring countries hosting refugees, as well as for those in need remaining inside Syria, to fulfill these commitments as quickly as possible, and to be responsive to future appeals, as the United States will be.

The spillover of the Syrian conflict, including terrorist attacks in Beirut, has weakened Lebanon's tourism sector, investment, and foreign trade—all important components of Lebanon's open economy. Uncertainty has depressed consumption, with wealthy tourists gone and more Lebanese reluctant to spend. Investors are delaying decisions, and Lebanon's land trade routes have been disrupted. This year will likely be the fourth consecutive year of slowing growth for the Lebanese economy. For example, the World Bank has estimated that the crisis will cut real GDP growth in Lebanon by 2.9 percent this year.

Our economic assistance programs encourage growth in Lebanon through improving the technical expertise of small businessowners and their access to financial resources, especially in the agricultural sector. We also encourage the Lebanese Government to do more to promote economic reform, including privatization of its moribund public sector industries, though this has been stymied due to political gridlock.

Banking is a pillar of the Lebanese economy, and the banking sector, despite all of Lebanon's economic challenges, saw deposits grow significantly in 2013, providing economic stability through its purchases of government debt and funding of private sector activity. Given its importance, it is all the more critical that the banking sector in Lebanon safeguard Lebanon's place in the international financial system by doing all it can to protect itself and correspondent banks in the United States and elsewhere from money laundering and terrorist finance. In coordination with the Treasury Department, we engage with the Central Bank of Lebanon and with Lebanese banks to ensure that they have vigorous systems to combat these illicit finance threats.

The most promising economic sector in the medium- to long-term may be the hydrocarbons industry. Lebanon may have substantial reserves of offshore natural gas and maybe even oil deposits. However, the lengthy political stalemate, as well as a maritime boundary dispute with Israel, has prevented Lebanon from further exploring its offshore resources. As a result, no exploration has taken place, and any potential finds would take a number of years to begin producing.

We expect the newly formed Cabinet may take steps to restart the process to allow international oil companies to enter the Lebanese market and explore. The State Department is engaging with both sides to explore potential solutions to the maritime boundary dispute. Those discussions have progressed well, and we hope they will resume with the new government now in place.

THE IMPORTANCE OF BROAD INTERNATIONAL SUPPORT

In the face of all these challenges, U.N. Secretary General Ban Ki-moon and President Michel Sleiman mobilized support for Lebanon's stability, sovereignty, and state institutions by launching last September the International Support Group for Lebanon, which currently consists of the U.N., the permanent members of the U.N. Security Council, the World Bank, the Arab League, Germany, Italy, and the EU. It was a strong demonstration of international support for Lebanon's sovereignty and stability, and for responsible Lebanese political actors.

We look to the ISG to be an active vehicle by which the international community can demonstrate political and financial support to promote stability and to help Lebanon address specific challenges. Secretary Kerry will attend the next gathering of the ISG in just 8 days, in Paris.

The United States, along with many others in the international community, is committed to ensuring an end to the era of impunity for assassinations and political violence in Lebanon. That is why we strongly support the work of the Special Tribunal for Lebanon. One month ago, the Tribunal began its initial trials to bring to justice those responsible for assassinating former Prime Minister Rafik Hariri in 2005, along with dozens of innocents killed in this and other attacks. The Lebanese people deserve accountability and justice. The commencement of the trials is an important step, but political violence still plagues Lebanon. Former Finance Minister and Ambassador to the United States Mohammad Chatah was assassinated in December in downtown Beirut. Two other March 14 leaders survived assassination attempts in 2012—a minister in the current Cabinet, Boutros Harb, and Lebanese Forces leader Samir Geagea. ISF Information Branch Chief Wissam al-Hassan was killed in a car bomb in Beirut in October 2012.

Chairman Kaine, Ranking Member Risch, Members: Lebanon has faced many existential challenges since gaining independence in 1943, and today it faces similar challenges from the war in Syria. Lebanon has found reliable international partners to see it through some of its darkest periods and emerge the stronger for it. The 1989 Taif Accord was the basis for ending 15 years of civil war, and its multiconfessional National Pact remains in effect. U.N. Security Council Resolutions 1559 and 1701 helped structure a return to stability. The 2012 Baabda Declaration established the principle that all Lebanese parties and factions should abstain from regional conflicts. It needs to be implemented by all parties.

But Lebanon has friends, and the United States is one of them. We need to stand with the people of Lebanon; it is in our national interest to promote a stable, secure, and sovereign Lebanon, one that is free of foreign interference and that is able to defend its own interests. And we will continue our efforts to end the conflict in Syria, as that conflict—left unchecked—will, among other repercussions, continue to destabilize Lebanon and other states in the region.

Senator KAINE. Thank you, Mr. Silverman.

General Plehn.

STATEMENT OF MAJ. GEN. MICHAEL T. PLEHN, PRINCIPAL DIRECTOR FOR MIDDLE EAST POLICY, OFFICE OF THE SECRETARY OF DEFENSE, U.S. DEPARTMENT OF DEFENSE, WASHINGTON, DC

General PLEHN. Thank you, sir. Chairman Kaine, thank you for the opportunity to speak today, and thank you for your help in drawing attention to Lebanon's security challenges, especially those due to the Syrian conflict. The impact on Lebanon from the conflict in Syria has become acute, as you well know, and you have described the impact of the refugees, as has Mr. Silverman as well.

But the Syrian conflict also is attracting foreign fighters from across the region and around the world. Those foreign fighters are becoming battle-hardened and gaining experience that could have destabilizing effects in the years to come.

Of great concern—and you have mentioned it already—the Islamic State of Iraq and the Levant, in particular, has exploited the growing governing vacuum in eastern Syria to carve out territory to train its fighters, recruit more fighters, and plan attacks. Both the ISIL and al-Nusra Front have established a presence in Lebanon and are seeking to increase their cooperation with Sunni extremist groups already operating in Lebanon. And as you noted, during your recent visit the Sunni terrorist attacks in Lebanon certainly are on the rise.

Since 2014, seven attacks against Shia population centers have been executed. Approximately 10 individuals have died and more than 120 have been wounded in those attacks.

I would tell you that the Lebanese Armed Forces have taken a variety of bold measures to maintain stability in Lebanon and counter the destabilizing effects that the Syrian conflict risks to Lebanon's security. The increased operational tempo of Lebanese Armed Forces' deployments over the past few months reflects their commitment to Lebanon's security. In fact, the last willingness to exercise its role as the sole, legitimate defense force in Lebanon has made it a target as well, and just last weekend, second border regiment personnel were killed when a suicide bomber detonated a vehicle near an LAF checkpoint.

I would also tell you that our continued engagement and assistance to Lebanon and the Lebanese Armed Forces is all the more important in this time of increased challenges to Lebanon's stability. As mentioned in previous testimony, the Lebanese have just agreed upon a new government. This important step provides us with an opportunity to increase our engagements both with Lebanon's Government as a whole and the Lebanese Armed Forces in particular.

For fiscal year 2014, we have provided approximately $71 million in foreign military financing, thanks to the U.S. Congress, and $8.7 million in fiscal year 2013 1206 funding. Both of those strengthen the capacity of the Lebanese Armed Forces and support its mission to secure Lebanon's borders, defend the sovereignty of that state, and implement, as Mr. Silverman noted, U.N. Security Council Resolutions 1559 and 1701.

Since 2005, the United States has allocated nearly $1 billion to support the Lebanese Armed Forces and internal security forces, making us Lebanon's key partner in security cooperation.

Recently in December 2013, President Suleiman announced the Saudi Arabia will grant Lebanon $3 billion to purchase defense items from the French. So in concert with international partners such as the French and in line with the International Support Group for Lebanon that Mr. Silverman mentioned, we fully support strengthening the Lebanese Armed Forces and will continue to work with partners to ensure our assistance is complementary and used effectively to meet these growing challenges.

I would also tell you that our International Military Education and Training program with Lebanon is our fourth-largest in the world. It builds strong ties between the United States and Lebanon by bringing Lebanese officers to the United States. In fiscal year 2013, Lebanon received $2.9 million under the IMET program. That allowed 67 Lebanese military students to attend education and training classes here in the United States. Since 1985, this program has brought more than 1,000 Lebanese military students to the United States for education and training.

Similarly, our section 1206 assistance has enabled the LAF to monitor, secure, and protect Lebanon's borders against terrorist threats and the illicit transfer of goods. Since 2006, the United States has provided more than $100 million in section 1206 to assist the LAF.

We are also focused on the LAF's desire for institutional reform. The DOD has just instituted a defense institution reform initiative with the LAF. This initiative complements a U.S. whole-of-government effort supporting Lebanese security sector reform.

In closing, sir, I would say that our positive relationship with and continued support to Lebanon and the Lebanese Armed Forces is now more important than ever. And I thank you and the other distinguished members of your subcommittee for not only calling this hearing but for your abiding interest and support for Lebanon. Thank you.

[The prepared statement of General Plehn follows:]

PREPARED STATEMENT OF MAJ. GEN. MICHAEL PLEHN

Chairman Kaine, Ranking Senator Risch, and other distinguished members of the subcommittee, I appreciate the opportunity to speak to you today about the evolving security situation in Lebanon in relation to the conflict in Syria and the importance of our partnership with the Lebanese Armed Forces.

Your help in drawing attention to Lebanon's security challenges, especially to those due to the Syrian conflict, is both timely and beneficial.

The impact on Lebanon from the conflict in Syria has become acute. In Lebanon, there are now nearly 1 million refugees from Syria, equal to approximately 20-percent of the current population in Lebanon. Despite Lebanon's official dissociation policy regarding the Syrian conflict, Hezbollah is militarily involved in Syria, and sectarian tensions are spilling over the Syria-Lebanon border. Lebanese towns and villages near the border with Syria regularly experience shelling from Syria—both by the Syrian regime and Syrian opposition forces—due to regime allegations that opposition fighters use Sunni-dominated areas as safe havens as well as opposition allegations that Hezbollah uses Shia-dominated areas to enter Syria and launch attacks.

The Syrian conflict is attracting foreign fighters from across the region and around the world. We assess there are now significantly more foreign fighters in Syria than there were foreign fighters in Iraq at the height of the Iraq war. Many of these fighters are finding their way to a number of fighting units, including terrorist groups such as the al-Nusra Front, and the Islamic State of Iraq and the Levant. These foreign fighters are becoming battle-hardened and gaining experience that could have destabilizing effects in the years to come. Of great concern, the Islamic State of Iraq and the Levant, in particular, has exploited the governing vacuum in eastern Syria to carve out territory to train its fighters, recruit more of them, and plan attacks. Both the Islamic State of Iraq and the Levant and al-Nusra Front have established a presence in Lebanon and are seeking to increase their cooperation with Sunni extremists groups already operating in Lebanon. These Lebanese-based groups have claimed a number of recent attacks in Lebanon.

Senator Kaine, as you experienced during your recent visit to Beirut, Sunni terrorist attacks in Lebanon are on the rise. Since the beginning of 2014 alone, seven suicide attacks have hit Shia population centers. Last week's twin bombing in Bir Hassan, as reported in the press, likely was targeting the Iranian Culture Center in the area in south Beirut. Approximately 10 individuals died and more than 120 were wounded. The al-Qaeda-linked Abdallah Azzam Brigades claimed responsibility for the attacks. Leaders across Lebanon's political spectrum have condemned the attacks.

THE LEBANESE ARMED FORCES AND STABILITY

The Lebanese Armed Forces has taken a variety of bold measures to maintain stability in Lebanon and counter the destabilizing effects that the Syrian conflict risks to Lebanon's security. The increased operational tempo of Lebanese Armed Forces deployments over the past few months reflects their commitment to Lebonon's security. In the last 7 months, we have seen our partners in the Lebanese Special forces deploy to Sidon for counterterrorism operations, to Tripoli to conduct stability operations, and to Arsal to provide security for the populations affected by Syria's instability. Throughout this period, the 2nd Intervention Regiment conducted stability operations and supported counterterrorism and counternarcotics efforts in the Bekaa Valley. The LAF's willingness to exercise its role as the sole legitimate defense force in Lebanon has made it a target as well. Just last weekend, 2nd Border Regiment personnel were killed when a suicide bomber detonated his vehicle at a LAF checkpoint.

U.S. and international assistance builds the capacity of the Lebanese Armed Forces to serve the democratic government and people of Lebanon. The Lebanese Armed Forces have organized themselves effectively to maintain a tremendously high operational tempo for many of its units, and have demonstrated the ability to make appropriate requests for and use of equipment, as well as unity and professionalism in numerous operations. One recent example of the Lebanese Armed Forces' success was the February 12, 2014, arrest of an Abdallah Azzam official, which led to the discovery of and dismantling of a large car bomb.

U.S. SUPPORT TO THE LEBANESE ARMED FORCES

Our continued engagement and assistance to the Lebanese Armed Forces are all the more important in this time of increased challenges to Lebanon's stability. As mentioned in previous testimony, the Lebanese have just agreed upon a new government formed by Prime Minister Tammam Salam. This is an important step for the government and people of Lebanon, and provides us with an opportunity to increase our engagement with Lebanon's Government as a whole and the Lebanese Armed Forces in particular.

The emergence of the Lebanese Armed Forces as Lebanon's sole legitimate defense force is a critical component of Lebanon's long-term stability and development. U.S. assistance to Lebanese Armed Forces, approximately $71 million in fiscal year 2014 FMF and $8.7M in fiscal year 2013 1206 funding, strengthens the capacity of the Lebanese Armed Forces and supports its mission to secure Lebanon's borders, defend the sovereignty of the state, and implement U.N. Security Council Resolutions 1559 and 1701. Since 2005, the United States has allocated nearly $1 billion to support the Lebanese Armed Forces and Internal Security forces, making us Lebanon's largest partner in security cooperation—a key pillar of our bilateral relationship.

In December 2013, President Sleiman announced that Saudi Arabia will grant Lebanon $3 billion to purchase defense items from the French. In concert with international partners such as the French, and in line with the International Support Group for Lebanon, we fully support strengthening the Lebanese Armed Forces and will continue to work with partners to ensure that our assistance is complementary and used effectively to meet these growing challenges.

Our International Military Education and Training (IMET) program with Lebanon is the 4th-largest in the world. IMET builds strong ties between the United States and Lebanon by bringing Lebanese officers and officials to the United States for professional development and to train alongside U.S. forces. In fiscal year 2013, Lebanon received $2.9M under the IMET program that allowed 67 Lebanese military students to attend education and training classes in the United States. Since 1985, the IMET program has brought more than 1,000 Lebanese military students to the United States for education and training.

Our Section 1206 assistance has enhanced the Lebanese Armed Forces' ability to monitor, secure, and protect Lebanon's borders against terrorist threats and the illicit transfer of goods. Since 2006, the United States has provided more than $100M in Section 1206 funding to assist the Lebanese Armed Forces to build its counterterrorism capabilities. Most recently, Congress approved $9.3M in FY 2014 1206 funding to enhance Lebanon's border security capability further by providing the Lebanese Armed Forces' 2nd Border Regiment with additional surveillance equipment to guard its portion of the border—including radars, seismic sensors, and cameras.

We are also focused on supporting the Lebanese Armed Forces' desire for institutional reform; the Department of Defense has just started a Defense Institution Reform Initiative (DIRI) with the Lebanese Armed Forces. This initiative complements a U.S. whole-of-government effort supporting Lebanese security sector reform. U.S. Central Command continues to provide support to the training and professionalization of the Lebanese Armed Forces, while the Department of State Bureau of International Narcotics and Law Enforcement Affairs funds a program to strengthen the capability and management capacity of the Internal Security Forces. All of these programs help to strengthen our relationship and ties between our two militaries and throughout their ranks.

SUPPORTING LEBANON

The crisis in Syria will likely not end soon, nor unfortunately will its impact on neighboring Lebanon. Our positive relationship with, and continued support to, Lebanon and the Lebanese Armed Forces is now more important than ever. The effectiveness of U.S. security assistance to the Lebanese Armed Forces is evident in how well it has managed the violence that has plagued Lebanon over the course of the conflict in Syria. The Lebanese Armed Forces is a critical pillar of Lebanon's stability and its ability and commitment to curtailing sectarian fighting and terrorism has been a significant factor in preventing Lebanon from descending into greater violence.

Senator KAINE. I just cannot help but comment that only the acronym ''happy''—the U.S. military could use the phrase ''LAF'' with a straight face. Lebanese Armed Forces. I am sure everyone knows that, but even the armed forces gave me a hat with LAF on it that I am now wearing around.

So let me just ask you first. When we went to Lebanon—for either or both of you—a lot of what we heard before we went was the warning that Lebanon is approaching a breaking point, and that would be described differently by different people asking that. Is that kind of language alarmist or accurate?

Mr. SILVERMAN. Mr. Chairman, I would say we do not quite use that language only because Lebanon has been through so much, more than maybe arguably any other country. But this is a very, very serious situation, and Lebanon is facing very, very serious threats. It faced threats even before the Syrian war to its independence and its sovereignty and its security obviously. There were political assassinations before the Syrian conflict, for example. But the Syrian conflict has really exacerbated this.

The Lebanese are fond of using an Arabic word that translates into ''saturation'' when they talk about the refugee issue, that they are saturated. In other words, even though you could give more money—the international community can and should give more money, but they are simply saturated as a society with this. But we are appreciative that they are reaching out and accepting these people.

But I would say there are real risks and threats, and that is why it is so important that the international community get behind the moderate, the responsible voices in Lebanon, that are very concerned about threats to stability.

Senator KAINE. General Plehn, any thoughts on that question?

General PLEHN. Yes, sir. I would say that Lebanon has proven to be amazingly resilient, given the stresses that they have been put under certainly from what has been happening in Syria as well. And I think a key component of that resilience, at least on the military side with the Lebanese Armed Forces, has been that engagement between the United States and the Lebanese Armed Forces. They have shown some very good progress recently certainly in counterterrorism fronts as well.

Thank you.

Senator KAINE. We spent time with the new Prime Minister talking about the formation of the government. And the system and the steps over the next couple of months are a little bit unusual, and I wanted to get your opinions about what might likely occur. We are nearing the end of a 6-year Presidential term, and the expectation is there would be Presidential elections by late May. If there is a successful Presidential election, the newly formed Prime Minister and government would then dissolve after 3 months. But I gather they would dissolve with the feeling that they had done their job, and depending on how the Presidential election goes, there is some chance that that Cabinet and Prime Minister could be the nucleus of the next government working together with a new President. Am I reading this the right way?

Mr. SILVERMAN. You are, Mr. Chairman.

One other comment on your first question, just to echo what General Plehn just said, which is this is a very tough situation. It could be much worse and much tougher had we not had the institution of the Lebanese Armed Forces and the internal security forces to help, assisted by us and the development of this relationship.

This is a unique—it is an overused word. I think this is a unique political situation. So the government now has to try to reach agreement on a ministerial statement. If it does not, it goes on being a caretaker, which means it is not able to make—even before the Presidential election—is not able to make real policy. And some of these economic decisions, which tend to get lost—if the government does not, for example, pass decrees, it cannot issue tenders for this gas exploration, for example. And these are issues that generally have not been taken up by caretaker governments. That is why they need to have a fully empowered government to do that.

And as you say, it may be that if we can take the spirit that reached this compromise to reach a government, if that extends to the Presidential election, then we have a President. Then we will have another government. Hopefully that would be easier to form, given that we have gone through a government fully empowered or a vote of confidence and a Presidential election.

But there is no sugar coating. This gets down to a very complicated process in which a lot of equities have to be taken into account. And as you see, one day there is going to be a government, the next day there will not be a government. And we thought that we might have a ministerial statement even yesterday. Now we are waiting for them. I hope they can reach agreement on that. So I hope that we can build upon what spirit we have had in reaching the formation of a government.

Senator KAINE. The selection of the President is also different than we might think of it here. The selection of the President is done by Parliament based on a two-thirds vote. It is not automatic that you get a two-thirds vote for a President. We were in dialogue with local leaders, and one of the possibilities they indicated was that in the past, when it has been difficult to find a candidate who could reach the two-thirds threshold, that there would be a temporary adjustment of the constitution to allowing the sitting President to have a holdover period. It might be a year. It might be 2 years.

We met with President Suleiman and he certainly did not suggest anything about staying past his 6-year term.

But based on what you know now, what do you think is the prospect that by May there could be the candidates who could come out who might be able to develop a two-thirds support in a Parliament for the selection of a new President post-late May?

Mr. SILVERMAN. No. You are exactly right, Mr. Chairman. And I cannot put a percentage on the possibility that this will happen. We believe it is important to do these elections, which are parliamentary not popular elections, on time and according to the constitution. You are right. They have gotten around this before by extension of the President. I do not know if that will happen. The intent right now is to truly elect a President. And there are different means of electing a President, whether you work it out and bring it as more of kind of a rubber stamp by the Parliament or you have a genuine debate within Parliament. We do not know exactly what will happen. So it is really very, very difficult to guess at this point. I would say the odds increased of an election of a President, but who knows? And just the add to the complexity, then we would have another government. Then it would have to form itself up.

And remember, we are looking at parliamentary elections again later this year because this Parliament will go out of business in November just based on the previous extension of its mandate. We had wanted elections before, and I think the Lebanese wanted elections before but they were not able to organize parliamentary elections. So it is even more complicated than that. So this is a very eventful political year for Lebanon.

Senator KAINE. With Hezbollah openly declaring its support for Assad in Syria and sort of going all in to send troops in in Syria, how has that affected Hezbollah politically inside Lebanon? I know there has been controversy about that decision by Hezbollah to do that. It certainly has engendered acts of Sunni violence that have spiked, largely attributed to Hezbollah's decision to go all in in Syria. So talk about Hezbollah's political support in Lebanon and how the decision to focus on Syria has affected their political support?

Mr. SILVERMAN. As I said in my remarks, Mr. Chairman, this is not a war in which the people of Lebanon wanted or want to be involved. This is, in effect, Hezbollah dragging the people of Lebanon into a foreign war.

I think there have been political costs for Hezbollah in this. I cannot say if that is why we have a government today. I think there is a lot of concern across the board, across the political spectrum regarding the violence that you witnessed directly and that has plagued Lebanon of late but even more so than throughout its political life. So I think there have been political costs. And we will have to see. That is why elections are important. We will have to see how that manifests itself. You cannot automatically translate it, but I think there is deep-seated concern on the part of the Lebanese people that they are not getting anything out of this. As a matter of fact, everything that is flowing from this is negative for them, and it goes well beyond the refugee situation.

We have condemned the violence from Sunni extremists, as well as from Shia extremists. So Lebanon is paying a heavy price, and the Lebanese people deserve to stop being forced to pay that price.

Senator KAINE. In your testimony and in my opening comments, I talked a lot about the Syria effect on Lebanon, which was a main subject of virtually every conversation we had.

I want to ask a question about one other significant dynamic, the U.S. discussions with the P5+1 nations with Iran over their nuclear program and the prospect that a resolution of that particular challenge and some rapprochement between Iran and the United States or Iran and other nations, including Saudi Arabia, could have within Lebanon. Could a potential rapprochement with appropriate skepticism about whether we would get there between Iran and the West and Saudi Arabia open the door to greater political stability in Lebanon, or would there be a converse concern that an emboldened Iran freed from some of the sanctions might further exacerbate tensions in the country?

Mr. SILVERMAN. Thank you, Mr. Chairman.

I think if you talk to Lebanese people, a lot of Lebanese people would tell you that they would like to believe—genuinely like to believe—that if we are able to reach a nuclear deal—the P5+1 is able to reach a nuclear deal with Iran—that it will have a positive effect, not the negative effect. I hope that is not the case. But most people like to think that there is a possibility here.

Iran's regional actions are obviously a threat. We have condemned them. They are a state sponsor of terrorism, and they continue, obviously, to be a major supporter of the Assad regime, among many other aspects of sponsoring terrorism. But this is not part of the P5+1 talks. They are very much focused on the nuclear issue.

I hope that what you say is true and that it will induce Iran to adopt a more responsible behavior in the region. When it came to the Geneva conference and the issue came up over Iran coming, potentially attending, could Iran potentially be a part of a solution? Theoretically, yes; but we were asking it to do what everybody else that attended the Geneva conference was being asked to do, which was to accept the Geneva communique and the purpose of the Geneva talks which Iran chose not to do. And so Iran exempted itself—excepted itself from that process.

So hopefully it will have that more—if we are able—and the big "if" is we are able to reach an agreement. It will have that positive effect. Obviously, that is up to Iran, but I think in Lebanon, the Lebanese people want to see, obviously, a change in Iranian policy toward Lebanon, as well as to Syria.

Senator KAINE. Let me ask a question or two about refugees before turning to Lebanese Armed Forces questions for General Plehn.

One of the issues we picked up in dialogue with NGOs and the U.N. High Commissioner was sort of the changing definition of this refugee challenge. So the dimension from numbers is significant and sizable. If you assume that the refugee problem is a short-lived problem, you treat it one way, but once someone has lived in the country for a year and then 2 years and 3 years—I think there are about 330,000 young people in the Lebanese public school system, and there are nearly 75,000 or 80,000 Syrian children of school age who are now living in communities. As the refugee challenge goes on for longer and longer, the strategies for dealing with refugee issues start to change. You know, instead of emergency aid of water bottles, what do you do to develop better water systems?

Do you think our strategy and the strategy of the U.N. and other refugee-serving agencies is appropriately starting to look at sort of the long-term need or are we still focusing on the kind of emergency relief that might not really take into account the realistic nature of that refugee population?

Mr. SILVERMAN. Mr. Chairman, I think your diagnosis is exactly correct. As large and as bad as the figures are in terms of the total number of refugees that have come into Lebanon and to Jordan and elsewhere, in some sense the bigger number is how many years they might stay.

Senator KAINE. Right.

Mr. SILVERMAN. If you look at the region, Lebanon has raised this very real challenge with us. I do not know if you met with King Abdullah of Jordan when he was here.

Senator KAINE. Two weeks ago; yes.

Mr. SILVERMAN. But he has often spoken of this. It is this challenge of when might these people go home.

This is not something that comes new to us or is a new consideration. And that is why we talk about assistance to the refugees. We always need to make sure that people understand we are talking about assistance to the refugees and to the communities that are hosting them because even in Jordan, 80 percent of the refugees are not living in camps. And as you know, Lebanon has very restricted, informal tented settlements in a couple of places, but in general, no camps. There are 1,600 communities in which the refugees live.

So it is a huge strain on educational systems, and that has to be addressed. And some of our money is going to expanding access to education. When we say access for the refugees, we also mean access for the local communities because otherwise refugees are taking up that access. You have seen double sessions in school and things like that.

Senator KAINE. And just again for the audience—most may follow this, but it is pretty important to note—because of the number of Syrian children in Lebanon, many Lebanese schools are going to split shifts, morning sessions with refugee children and afternoon sessions with local populations or vice versa, often having to teach in different languages in the morning and afternoon sessions. So again, thinking 330,000 children in the public schools nationally, but about 80,000 refugee children in this community, the magnitude of this challenge is very, very dramatic.

Mr. SILVERMAN. So beyond the education issue are particular issues of health and infrastructure, meaning water infrastructure, for example, which is hugely important in Lebanon and in Jordan as well. And so some of our money is going to the U.N. and other money is going to NGOs. And Secretary Kerry, when he attended the International Support Group in New York in September, brought with him $30 million that was particularly focused on aiding the host communities. So we are dealing with water, trying to enhance and increase water infrastructure to get to these communities. And it can be helping with housing to be honest, money that is going to communities when they add on to their houses, for example, to accommodate refugees.

So absolutely, you are right to focus on these longer term infrastructural burdens because, as you mentioned earlier, you are getting a youth population. And as I think you heard when you were in Lebanon, a lot of kids just not being educated. Period. And that has enormous implications not just for Lebanon but throughout the region.

Senator KAINE. I gather that the way you describe this challenge, the International Support Group that was convened is looking at this dynamic where, instead of emergency relief, as the conflict in Syria stretches longer, they need to possibly change the kinds of relief they provide to the refugee and host populations.

Mr. SILVERMAN. Yes, that is right. We do not need to wait for groups, either an international support group or any other institution. We need to do it. The individual countries need to do it ourselves. And that is why we are focused on that. Our money is already focusing on that. And when we talk about Lebanon with our allies, we are talking about these kind of long-term challenges that need to be addressed, not just getting the immediate needs of food or medicine.

Senator KAINE. General Plehn, turning to the Lebanese Armed Forces, before I ask about the relationship with U.S. military, I would like your assessment on one sort of aspect of the Lebanese Armed Forces. You know, one of the clear challenges, as we met with civilian leadership, the complexity of forming a government in a population where there has been this tradition of very delicate power-sharing between Sunni, Shia, Maronite, Roman Catholic, different groups within the country. It is a little bit like Belgian politics where everything sort of has to be allocated not among language groups but among ethnic groups. And that, together with the complications of the Syrian civil war, was the reason it took so long to put together this governing coalition.

Moving over into the Lebanese Armed Forces, how are they able to integrate these populations? The civil side has a hard time doing it, but within the Lebanese Armed Forces, are the Sunni, Shia, and Christian service men and women well integrated in units? And can that serve a leadership function in terms of modeling to the remainder of society that, look, this can be done?

General PLEHN. Mr. Chairman, that is both a great question and a great observation, and you have highlighted certainly the difficulty within Lebanon with the many different confessions that come together in that country. What I would tell you is what you know, that the Lebanese Armed Forces really is a model for how those different confessions are able to come together within that country, certainly rally behind the mission of being the sole, legitimate security provider for the country itself and then I think, as you noted, provide that model for the rest of the country for the future.

Senator KAINE. Talk a little bit about how the Lebanese Armed Forces responds to these twin challenges, first of having this sizable and powerful militia in Hezbollah and, second, now that there is this spike in Sunni-Shia violence since Hezbollah has gone into Syria. These are two different kinds of challenges that the Lebanese Armed Forces have to deal with. Talk a little bit about their capacity in dealing with these two challenges, the Hezbollah relationship and the spike in Sunni-Shia violence in the last year or so.

General PLEHN. Yes, sir. If I may take the last first with the spike in Sunni-Shia violence. I think what we have seen is exactly what you would hope and expect out of any armed forces for a country, is that those individuals are willing to put themselves on the forefront of the fighting. And as I noted earlier in my testimony and as you noted as well, the Lebanese Armed Forces have paid the cost of that intervention to provide security for the people of Lebanon.

You, yourself, noted that Lebanese Hezbollah is a well-armed militia, something that just is not normal to us in America in terms of a construct for how we deal with armed force. Certainly from the United States military perspective, our engagement with the Lebanese Armed Forces to build that professional military force, to reinforce both to them and to the people of Lebanon that they are the sole, legitimate security provider for Lebanon is certainly that path that we want to go down.

Mr. SILVERMAN. Mr. Chairman, may I just jump on what Mike just said?

Senator KAINE. Yes, please.

Mr. SILVERMAN. Which is, there is another component too with the diplomatic component, which is we have to work together with governments in the region and even in Europe to stop the flow of foreign fighters going to this conflict. And we have to stop the flow of financing to violent extremists. And that is a very important effort that is going on right now. We have seen some steps by some countries to constrict or restrict and to penalize—punish with harsh laws, harsh penalties—people who go over to fight, who are going over to Syria or anywhere else to fight. And that really needs to be an important part of our whole-of-government approach to this problem. And I think it will be a subject, for example, when President Obama goes to Saudi Arabia later. That will be because we are working with all of the governments of the region and in Europe as well to deal with this. We really need to stop at the source as well.

Senator KAINE. If we hope to increase the support we provide to the Lebanese Armed Forces, how can we assure that any technological capacity or weapons systems or weaponry—that there are appropriate safeguards and accountability controls over U.S.-supplied security material so that they stay in the right hands and do not fall into the wrong hands in the middle of a very volatile security environment?

General PLEHN. Mr. Chairman, in Lebanon, much as we have in many other countries, we have an office of defense cooperation in Beirut. Their primary purpose truly is to ensure that we have the appropriate safeguards and that we are performing the appropriate end-use monitoring is what we call it when we provide foreign military sales, equipment to partner nations. So our U.S. personnel in the Office of Defense Cooperation in Beirut will do that enhanced end-use monitoring to ensure that that equipment is both accounted for and being used properly.

Senator KAINE. I found it interesting, in the dialogue with the Lebanese Armed Forces, their take on the Saudi Arabian and French potential for receipt of Saudi Arabian assistance to purchase French military assets. They said they liked the U.S. equipment a lot better basically is what the Lebanese Armed Forces was saying.

But I gather from your testimony, General, that you feel like the more partners, the better, the more assistance, the better. You do not find that Saudi Arabian provision of $3 billion to purchase French assistance—you do not find that troubling or problematic. You view it as greater partners to help the armed forces is to be desired and not to be feared?

General PLEHN. Sir, I think Lebanon can use a lot of friends right now. They are in difficult straits, as you well know. I would tell you that we certainly are working with Lebanon and with the rest of our partners, as I mentioned in my testimony, to ensure that that $3 billion grant is complementary to other efforts and that it is used on the things that the Lebanese Armed Forces truly need the most. I would offer to you that there are infrastructure-type projects that would help support the Lebanese Armed Forces that would be as, if not more, valuable to them in many areas than specific pieces of equipment.

Senator KAINE. Thank you for that answer.

One more question about the economy, back to Mr. Silverman. You talked about the prospects for natural gas to be a boost for the Lebanese economy. It requires more than a caretaker government to make some of the decisions about accessing those oilfields, which I guess would largely be in the Mediterranean. But could you expand a little bit on what these natural gas reserves might offer Lebanon and how those could help the Lebanese economy?

Mr. SILVERMAN. We do not know exactly how large they are, but there is significant interest and they could be extensive. Obviously, Israel is on the other side of this, and their resources are extensive, what they have found so far, as you know. So I think the interest is there, and it really could be a great, great boon to the Lebanese economy. There is no question about it if it is handled the right way and if they get in and move forward because this is not a static market.

I am not the expert, but the experts that work on this have explained to me and to the Lebanese that there are a finite number of investments. There is a finite amount of money that the international oil companies have to invest. And they will see a potentially profitable field, but they also need to have the certainty or the confidence that they can put in a major, major investment, not the investment to do an initial exploration or something, which may not be very much. But when you really get in and sign contracts and move forward with exploitation, that is an enormous investment. And meanwhile, other countries are attracting these companies, and Lebanon is behind because it cannot attract because it cannot release a tender.

So I think it is hard to put a figure on how much it could contribute to the GDP of Lebanon, but I think everyone acknowledges that it could be quite significant if the structure is put together, the regulatory structure too, and the exploration moves forward.

Senator KAINE. And is one of the issues with Lebanon—I think there are two sizable fields in the Mediterranean, one pretty much in what all would agree are Israeli waters and one that kind of straddles a border, depending on how you draw the water border, between Israel and Lebanon. I gather the exploitation of that field would probably not just require a Lebanese non-caretaker government to decide to move forward, but possibly also some cooperation with the Israeli Government about making sure that those borders are appropriately delineated.

Mr. SILVERMAN. I referred in my remarks to this maritime boundary line and, Senator, you are exactly correct. That is what we are talking about here. The companies, obviously, make this judgment themselves, but when I said they are looking for certainty and predictability, they do not want to enter a political dispute. They do not want to enter in a territory that will then turn out to be still subject to a dispute. And that is why we have been talking to both the Israelis and to the Lebanese trying to be helpful in reaching a solution to their maritime boundary line and what can be exploited. We think it can be done. We absolutely believe that there can be an arrangement worked out and that Lebanon can go forward if the decisions are made.

Senator KAINE. I have about 5 hours more of questions for this panel, but I do want to get to the second panel. Before I say a few concluding words and introduce the panel, I did want to at least pass to Senator Risch.

Senator RISCH. Thank you. I will pass.

Senator KAINE. Let me just say a word in conclusion. One of the most powerful aspects of this visit—and I have got a State Department witness and a DOD witness here today. But one of the most powerful aspects of the trip was going to the memorial to U.S. men and women from our State Department, from our military, who lost their lives in Lebanon, and the list of people is very, very long. I think Senator King and I were really struck looking at the memorial, the Marine barracks bombing, the Embassy bombing, the Embassy Annex bombing, and then a whole series of other instances, two, three, four, five, six, seven Americans at a time during that period in the early 1980s, the late 1980s. It was a very powerful thing. It was a very visible indication not only of American sacrifice but of the kinds of challenges that that very resilient Lebanese population has been dealing with on a daily basis.

But it also made Senator King and I really step back and realize the sacrifice that our military and our Foreign Service—sometimes we do not express the same appreciation to nonmilitary who are serving abroad as ambassadors with a small "A" for us. That memorial makes very vivid the sacrifice of any Americans who serve abroad, whether in the military and other capacity. It is important that we acknowledge that. And I just wanted to acknowledge that as you finish.

There may be additional questions from members of the panel that will be submitted in writing. But I appreciate you being here today and look forward to continuing to shed some light on the situation in Lebanon with your help. Thank you very much for coming.

Let me now introduce our second panel. Our second panel will come up to the table with nametags ready.

Dr. Paul Salem is vice president of the Middle East Institute leading an initiative on Arab transitions. Prior to joining the Middle East Institute, Dr. Salem was the founding director of the Carnegie Middle East Center in Beirut, Lebanon, between 2006 and 2013 where he built a regional think tank distinguished by the quality of policy research and high regional profile. From 1999 to 2006, Dr. Salem was the director of the Fares Foundation and in 1989 founded and directed the Lebanese Center for Policy Studies, Lebanon's leading public policy think tank. Dr. Salem writes regularly in the Arab and Western press and has been published in numerous journals and newspapers. Dr. Salem, we are glad to have you today.

In addition, we have with us Mr. Aram Nerguizian, who is a senior fellow at the Center for Strategic and International Studies where he conducts research on strategic and military dynamics in the Middle East and north Africa. During his time at CSIS, Mr. Nerguizian has worked on Hezbollah and the Lebanese Armed Forces extensively. He is frequently consulted by governments and the private sector, appears regularly on television, and has authored a number of books and reports on the Middle East and regional security issues.

I would like to ask Dr. Salem to begin with his opening comments, followed by Mr. Nerguizian. Your written comments are accepted for the record. If you could try to summarize in about 5 minutes, and then we will move into a dialogue.

Dr. Salem.

STATEMENT OF DR. PAUL SALEM, VICE PRESIDENT, MIDDLE EAST INSTITUTE, WASHINGTON, DC

Dr. SALEM. Senator Kaine, Ranking Member Risch, thank you very much for the honor of sharing my views with you on my native Lebanon.

Lebanon is, indeed, at a crossroads both in time and space. What I mean by that, it has survived 3 years of the Syrian crisis. Can it survive a fourth and a fifth? The pressures in time are increasing at all levels. In space, it is at a crossroads in the sense that Lebanon is very much penetrated by regional and international influence, and Middle East is going through an intense period of restructuring not only in Syria but also as the United States sort of retreats slightly, the United States, Iran, the gulf countries and so on and Russia playing new games, Lebanon is very vulnerable to all of that. Lebanon has survived 3 years of the Syrian conflict, but for all of those 3 years has been close to the breaking point. Indeed, unless a resolution is achieved in the Syrian war, Lebanon's political and security institutions, its economy, and social fabric might, indeed, increasingly fall apart.

Lebanon is the weakest link in Syria's environment. Any investment in Lebanon is, indeed, an investment in regional stability and, I would say, global security.

The spillover from Syria is enormous. Lebanese politics has been aligned for, and against, the Assad regime for 9 years, and that has sort of defined political alliances in the country for a very long time. And that has created political paralysis, political tension in the country for the past 3 years.

The refugee situation is well known, and the numbers really go into uncharted territory. I know of no other country that has received so many refugees in such a short period of time. The first panel said are we close to the breaking point. This is uncharted territory. No society has done what Lebanon is attempting to do.

Now, on the other hand, Lebanon does have coping mechanisms. It is not a coincidence that it has survived for 3 years. It is a country accustomed to crisis and has been through many internal and regional crises before. The political system, although weak and often dysfunctional, is also inclusive and is built on principles of accommodation and power-sharing and that is very important.

The army, although severely challenged and viewed by some with some taint, remains a very important national and inclusive institution.

And the living memory of Lebanon's own civil war that ended in 1990 deters most parties and most citizens from moving toward any major confrontation.

As we know, a major step forward was taken 10 days ago with the formation of a national unity government. This is an extremely important step. It is the first step forward in 3 years. For the past year, there have been attempts to form a government, but let us not forget that for 2 years before that, since January 2011, Lebanon was limping along with a lopsided government which did not include the March 14 coalition. So after 3 years, this is indeed an extremely important step.

Certainly this new government deserves important support, endorsement, and cooperation. It needs to be followed right away with a Presidential election. Presidential elections require, yes, a two-thirds majority for a quorum. It requires a two-thirds majority in the first vote, but in the second vote, requires a simple majority. So it is not exactly as difficult as imagined. Extending the term of the President or changing the constitution—that in itself requires a two-thirds majority. So it is equally difficult, but you can elect a President with a simple majority after you get the first two-thirds quorum. There are hopes that in the accommodation that happened in the last few weeks this might be the case.

And I will indicate—we can come back to it later—that the change is not so much only internal bargaining and so on. There has been a change in the regional environment. The two main patrons of the two groups, Iran and Saudi Arabia—I think there has been a shift there certainly on the Saudi side. The fact that there has been a Geneva meeting—we can get back to that—but there has been a shift in the region. That might help us move forward in Lebanon.

Of course, we need to follow Presidential elections with parliamentary elections, as mentioned before.

On extremist groups, it is important to start by saying that all the major parties, certainly Shia, Christian, Druze, are committed to power-sharing, are committed to stability, are committed to avoid internal warfare. There is no major movement toward internal conflict. There is no will for it. There is no plan for it.

But there is a very high tension because of Hezbollah's direct engagement in the war in Syria, and this has led to some radicalization in the Sunni street in Lebanon and some homegrown groups, but it has also encouraged groups from Syria and others related to al-Qaeda to take the fight to Hezbollah territory inside Lebanon and that is what we have seen in the last few months. I think this will remain a serious security concern for Lebanon but is not about to bring the house down. Hezbollah is in a deep rut in terms of its engagement in Lebanon and Syria, and that will affect its long-term viability and the strategic environment between Hezbollah and Israel, its main and original enemy.

The key goal, obviously, would be to end the crisis in Syria. The best way to help Lebanon is to do that, but that does not seem to be happening any time soon.

For Lebanon, I would reiterate what many of my colleagues have said. Endorse and support the new government. Support the election of a new President and the holding of parliamentary elections. Continue to take the lead generously in donation to Lebanon and to the refugee community. Build on strong U.S.-Lebanese military cooperation and relations, as well as encourage allies to do so as well. Work to maintain stability along the Lebanon-Israel border. We have seen just in the last 24 hours an Israeli attack on the border area between Lebanon and Syria. The borders between Lebanon and Israel have been stable since 2006. It is important to keep that the case, and certainly the United States can be important in that area.

Finally, I would also agree with Mr. Silverman that encouragement for Lebanon to move forward on the offshore oil/gas issue is important. We can talk more about that in the Q&A. It is not so much that it would immediately get any revenues to the Lebanese Treasury. This might take a full decade, but moving forward in that area would give confidence to the Lebanese themselves, would make major international companies and states have a stake in Lebanon's stability, and might be a very important source of stability and confidence in Lebanon moving forward, even if the revenues will take many, many years, if at all, to move forward.

Thank you.

[The prepared statement of Dr. Salem follows:]

PREPARED STATEMENT OF PAUL SALEM

Senator Kaine, members of the committee, I am honoured to share with you my thoughts on the political and security situation in my native Lebanon, the impact of the ongoing war in Syria, and what implications there may be for U.S. policy.

The precarious republic of Lebanon has survived 3 years of the Syrian conflict, but it has been teetering close to the breaking point. Unless a resolution or dramatic de-escalation is achieved in the Syrian war in the coming year, Lebanon's political and security institutions, its economy and its social fabric might begin to come apart.

SYRIA SPILLOVER

The number of registered Syrian refugees in Lebanon, a country of only 4 million people, is rapidly approaching the 1 million mark, with thousands more arriving every day. That is like the United States receiving an influx of 80 million refugees in 2 years. Sixty-five percent of these refugees are women and children. One in five of them are under the age of 4.

Lebanon has kept its borders open, and the country's communities have welcomed these refugees in their villages, neighborhoods, and local facilities. But the burden has been heavy and the cost high. There are now as many Syrian children as Lebanese in a school system that was barely able to keep up with its precrisis obligations. The strain on the health, water, electricity, housing, and public service infrastructure has been enormous.

The crisis has also impacted the economy, which has gone from healthy growth to contraction; and unemployment, especially in host communities, has climbed rapidly. Tensions between host and refugee populations in some areas are on the rise, and the strain has added to the political and sectarian tensions already present in the country.

COPING MECHANISMS

But Lebanon—a country not unaccustomed to crisis—also has remarkable coping mechanisms. The political system, although weak and often dysfunctional, is nonetheless inclusive, and is built on principles of accommodation and power-sharing. The army, although severely challenged during the present crisis, remains a national and inclusive institution. And the living memory of Lebanon's own 16-year civil war that only ended two decades ago, presents a strong antidote to any rush toward major internal conflict.

The main political coalitions in Lebanon—known as the March 14 and March 8 coalitions—have been aligned for and against the Assad regime for the past 10 years. And while their differences increased during the Syrian crisis, leading to political tension and institutional paralysis, neither side was interested in pursuing significant internal conflict. For the first 2 years of the crisis, Lebanon had a lopsided government in which the March 14 coalition was not represented; but even that government resigned a year ago, and the country limped along with only a caretaker government. Parliamentary elections scheduled last year, also were not held.

A major step forward was achieved 10 days ago, when the country's polarized political factions agreed to form an inclusive national unity government. This is an important step in easing sectarian and factional tensions, consolidating precarious national stability, and helping the country ride out the oncoming waves of instability emanating from Syria. This new government should receive rapid and strong international support and endorsement.

To further reinforce Lebanon's political institutions, this step needs to be followed by the election of a new President for the republic to a fresh 6-year term, as the current President's term ends in May. And this should be followed in the fall by overdue parliamentary elections.

A revival of Lebanon's democratic and inclusive political institutions is essential to giving Lebanese confidence in their own future, and to give Lebanon's friends and investors, confidence as well that Lebanon can pull through this latest crisis. Lebanon's precarious republic has survived external and internal wars before; with strong external support, it might survive this latest crisis as well.

EXTREMIST GROUPS

While the country's main parties have joined a national unity government, polarization among the communities continues, and risks to security mount. Lebanon's outgoing government had declared an official policy of neutrality and disengagement toward the Syrian conflict, but Hezbollah fully engaged in the fight alongside the Assad regime. And many in the Sunni community sympathised with the Syrian rebels, offering various forms of aid and assistance.

Although the country remained generally calm, intermittent eruptions of violence have racked the northern city of Tripoli, the southern town of Sidon, and several border towns such as Ersal in the eastern part of the country. A string of car-bombs targeting Shiite as well as Sunni neighborhoods have repeatedly threatened to push tensions to the boiling point.

In the face of a heavily armed and militant Hezbollah, the main Sunni parties and politicians have generally chosen accommodation not confrontation. This has left some of the Sunni street dissatisfied, and created space for the rise of more radical groups that want to challenge Hezbollah directly. Some of these are home-grown, such as the movement of Sheikh Ahmad al-Assir, but others are part of wider regional networks in Syria and elsewhere, such as the Abdullah Azzam Brigades that claimed responsibility for the latest bombings, Jubhat al-Nusra and other al-Qaeda linked groups.

The leader of the mainstream Sunni Future Movement has recently called on his community to renounce such radical jihadist groups, and the state's security apparatus is struggling to better secure the border and track down members of these cells and networks, but these security breaches are likely to continue intermittently. They will shake Lebanon's stability, but are unlikely to bring the whole house down.

WHAT CAN AND SHOULD THE UNITED STATES DO?

Address the Cause

The key goal, of course, is to go to the source, and try to end or dramatically de-escalate the raging conflict in Syria. The tepid international response over the past 3 years to the Assad regime's massacring of its own people, and the feeble support to the Free Syrian Army and the nonrebel groups, has convinced the Assad regime and his allies that they can prevail. It has also created an opportunity for the rise of more radical opposition groups. Without serious pressure, this conflict will be resolved neither on the battlefield nor on the negotiating table; it is likely to go on for a decade or even two, with unimaginable human suffering and incalculable consequences for the region and for global security.

The Assad regime has proved willing to fight to the last Syrian and would rather govern part of a devastated Syria than share power with others in a united Syria. And yet, when faced with a massive military threat, as that made by the U.S. last August, it has buckled and made major concessions. A regime that rules by force responds only to superior force. As long as that is not forthcoming in terms of serious military support to the Free Syrian Army or external military action, they will offer no major concessions.

The latest pledge from the Obama administration to increase support to the opposition is welcome, but is likely to be below the level that would seriously worry the Assad regime or alter the balance of power. And it is way below what Assad's allies are pouring into Syria in terms of men, money, and materiel. Unless the power calculations are changed dramatically, Assad is not going anywhere in the foreseeable future.

De-Escalation

If the Syrian conflict is not going to end soon, and a real transition is not currently viable, the alternative interim goal should be to at least de-escalate the conflict and focus on achieving cease-fires, getting aid to the millions of Syrians that need it, stabilizing as many parts of the country as possible, and limiting the zones of active warfare. When Lebanon fell apart in 1975, it took 15 years to patch it back together again. But during those 15 years, there were periods of intense civil war, but many years and zones of relative calm in which citizens could rebuild their lives and businesses, send their kids to school, and go about their daily life while the political order that had fallen apart awaited a new configuration.

The U.N. Security Council Resolution passed last week ordering warring parties in Syria to stop blocking the delivery of humanitarian aid is an important but long overdue step in putting people first. If no one is going to win this war anytime soon, the world must focus on de-escalating the fighting, delivering urgent aid, creating zones of stability and normalcy, and saving Syrian civilians.

For Lebanon a resolution or de-escalation of the Syrian conflict would mean that no new refugees would enter the country, and the million that are already there would begin to make their way back to Syria. And it would also allow a diminution of political and security tensions that keep the country on tenterhooks.

Support for Lebanon

But if the Syrian conflict will be neither resolved nor de-escalated, then Lebanon is in for a very dangerous ride in 2014 and 2015 and will need all the help it can get from the United States and other friends.

The United States and Lebanon have enjoyed many decades of warm relations reinforced by shared values and a large Lebanese American community. And the U.S. has been a strong supporter of the Lebanese Armed Forces and the biggest contributor to Lebanon's refugee relief needs. Among the ways that the U.S. could build on this support and help Lebanon survive the continuing storm are the following:

—Endorse and support the new national unity government.

—Encourage the Lebanese parties to move forward in electing a new President of the republic and in holding overdue parliamentary elections.

—Include Lebanon in high level visits of U.S. officials to the region.

—Continue to take the lead in donating and getting other nations to donate to the urgent and growing needs of the massive refugee population, with an immediate focus on the upcoming International Support Group for Lebanon meeting on March 5 in Paris.

—Build on long-standing U.S.-Lebanese military cooperation and work with other allies to bolster the capacities of the Lebanese Army and internal security forces.

—Continue to work with the Lebanese security forces to boost their counterterrorism capacities.

—Encourage and provide assistance to the new Lebanese Government to move forward with the delayed offshore gas bidding round; this would provide much-needed economic confidence, and help build a more promising economic future for the country's rising generations.

IN CLOSING

The Syrian war has devastated Syria and destabilized the entire region. Lebanon is the weakest link in the chain of countries around Syria. It has been the most generous in welcoming war-ravaged refugees and paid the highest cost in terms of its own stability and security. It deserves all the help you can offer. And any investment in Lebanon's stability, is an investment in regional stability, and in global security.

I thank you for your attention and for the opportunity to address your esteemed Committee.

Senator KAINE. Thank you, Dr. Salem.

Mr. Nerguizian.

STATEMENT OF ARAM NERGUIZIAN, SENIOR FELLOW, BURKE CHAIR IN STRATEGY, CENTER FOR STRATEGIC AND INTERNATIONAL STUDIES, WASHINGTON, DC

Mr. NERGUIZIAN. Chairman Kaine, Ranking Member Risch, and distinguished members of the subcommittee, thank you for the opportunity to speak to you today about Lebanon and the pressures it faces in the wake of the Syria crisis and broader instability across the Levant.

I have submitted a far longer written analysis that both explains and contextualizes what I am about to stay in depth, using open-source reporting and research conducted in field work in Lebanon. I fully understand how busy members and their staff are, but I hope that some of you will still be able to look to it for a level of detail that I cannot go into in this short statement, and I request that it be put into the official record.

Senator KAINE. Without objection.

Mr. NERGUIZIAN. Allow me to summarize some of the key points.

Syria's civil war and the Lebanon-Syria insecurity nexus now complicate and inform every aspect of sectarian and factional competition in Lebanon in ways that neither the Lebanese nor their regional and international allies seem to have fully accounted for. The conflict in Syria also defines how both the United States and Iran deal with their respective sets of interests, partners, and allies in Lebanon and the broader region.

Competing Lebanese factions have adopted diametrically opposing views on Syria, Iran, and Saudi Arabia. Anecdotal data from polling and field work all show deep divisions along Sunni-Shiite lines. Lebanon's Shia continue to view the Assad regime, Iran, and Hezbollah favorably while maintaining unfavorable views of Saudi

Arabia. Meanwhile, the country's Sunnis continue to maintain the opposite set of views relative to the country's Shia.

The pressure that Lebanon's Christians feel as a result of local and regional Sunni-Shia tension are also growing. Whether it is on Assad, Iran, Hezbollah, or Saudi Arabia, a significant portion of Lebanon's Christians remain divided about whether any of these regional and local actors can be viewed favorably or whether they could be trusted to make positive and stabilizing use of their influence in Lebanon.

Hezbollah's decision to commit to offensive military operations inside Syria in concert with Assad's forces is a preemptive war of choice in Syria that reflects its own narrow set of overlapping priorities in the country. These include the primacy of preserving the resistance axis with Iran, Hezbollah's sense that it can neither appease increasingly militant Lebanese Sunni political forces, nor reverse deepening regional Sunni-Shia tensions, and that Shia communal fears as a regional minority group increasingly inform a need to create strategic depth in Syria.

In 2014, Hezbollah's military priorities in Syria continue to center on its combat role east of the Bekaa Valley with a focus on strategically significant terrain such as the town of Qusayr and the Al-Qalamoun mountain range. Both remain critical to supply lines, and whoever controls them can shape the flow of aid, weapons, and personnel either to or from Syria. Hezbollah may have accurately calculated that moderate and urban Sunni factions and political forces would not, or could not, escalate in Syria, or by resorting to attacks against the militant group or the Lebanese Shia community. However, the rural Sunnis in the north and the Bekaa have always been a separate demographic, and Hezbollah actions in Syria may also dramatically accelerate major shifts currently underway within the Sunni community.

In 2014, Lebanon's mainly Sunni ruling north continues to maintain the highest overall and extreme poverty rates in the country, at levels in excess of 52 percent, or more than twice the national average. Dire socioeconomics and feelings of being underrepresented by traditional Sunni leadership have left northern Sunnis increasingly vulnerable to the recruitment efforts of militant and jihadi groups, including the Abdullah Azzam Brigades, Jabhat al-Nusra, and the Islamic State of Iraq and al-Sham.

Meanwhile, these shifts within Lebanon's Sunni community are taking place both alongside and because of acute demographic, socioeconomic, and security pressures from the influx of mainly Sunni displaced Syrians, now numbering more than 900,000 in Lebanon and centered in parts of the country with high poverty rates, poor education, health care, and other infrastructure.

While the scale of pressures on Lebanon and its people continues to grow, there are still a broad range of actors and institutions that seek to play a stabilizing role, and no institution has contributed more to relative stability than the Lebanese Armed Forces, or the LAF. The principal national security partner of the United States in Lebanon, the LAF has expanded from a force of 59,000 in 2010 to a force of some 65,500 in 2014, largely in an effort to stand up border protection forces, including the first and second border regiments, to deal with the pressures from Syria. The undermanning of conventional units has also proven to be a necessary evil to ensure as broad a national deployment as possible, totaling some 24,000 to 30,000 troops in the field.

As a result of the conflict, the LAF maintains three core national security priorities. These include creating a real-world security and border regime along the Lebanese-Syrian border, managing the risks of on-again/off-again violence and volatility along the U.N. Blue Line between Israel and Lebanon, and lastly conducting what the LAF calls high intensity internal stability and counterterrorism operations.

In many ways, the LAF's growing counterterrorism capabilities and the central role of LAF military intelligence and counterintelligence efforts increasingly define the U.S.-Lebanon military-to-military relationship. The LAF's growing ability to act on external intelligence, focus on dismantling groups like the Abdullah Azzam Brigades and similar militant and jihadi organizations, and the military's interdiction of IED, vehicle IED, and suicide attacks are key sources of even limited stability in a region in turmoil.

The LAF has worked hard to bring on line two border regiments to manage growing instability. This has included building up fixed Sanger-style observation posts that will be equipped with day and night electro-optical surveillance systems and anti-RPG netting and protection, along with other defensive countermeasures. The LAF hopes to build at least an additional eight fixed observation posts in 2014.

What the LAF needs now at the national level to push through its national security priorities is strong government leadership and political top cover. While Prime Minister Tammam Salam managed to form a Cabinet that includes both March 14 and March 8 coalitions and that enjoys broad international legitimacy, it still remains unclear at the end of February 2014 whether the new Cabinet would be capable of seizing on the LAF's momentum along the border.

Lastly, at the international level, the LAF and the Lebanese need countries like the United States and other donors and partners to support the military's development efforts, especially the LAF's capabilities development plan, the International Support Group for Lebanon, and the upcoming Rome conference to support the LAF.

I could go into far greater detail on all of these pressures, but I will leave them for the Q&A period. I thank you for your time and this opportunity.

[EDITOR's NOTE.—The prepared statement submitted by Mr. Nerguizian was too voluminous to include in the printed hearing but will be maintained in the permanent record of the committee. It can also be found at: http://csis.org/files/publication/140225l NerguizianlLebanonltestimony.pdf.]

Senator KAINE. Thank you, Mr. Nerguizian.

We will just start a dialogue and these will be questions that I will pose to either or both of you as we explore in more detail some of your testimony.

First, I would like each of your assessments about sort of what will likely happen in the next steps in the political process from the ministerial statement to the Presidential election, whether you think it is more likely that there will be Presidential candidates in the selection of a new individual for President or whether it might prove more probable that we would see an extension of President Suleiman's term. I do not want you to have to pin down with precision your percentage estimates of the chances, but I think it will be helpful for us as we think about our relationship, to get the sense of you as experts as to what you think the next steps in the political process are likely to—what are the results likely to be.

Dr. SALEM. Well, as I said, the formation of this government does reflect the change in some of the regional powers in their positioning and they have encouraged their allies to work together to form this government. I think the ministerial statement certainly takes a bit of time. There is a lot going on. There is a lot being negotiated, but I think they will come out with a ministerial statement.

I think this regionally supported mood to create some stability in Lebanon to keep Lebanon politically away from the conflict that is going on Syria even though Hezbollah mainly is involved there—I think this will continue in the immediate future. And I hope that that will impact a very heated, sort of behind-closed-doors discussion that started about the next President. It is not clear exactly who that will be but I think there is current momentum toward actually electing a next President. There is more leniency from both sides to accept a candidate even if that candidate is not their favorite candidate. None of the major players, maybe except one of the Christian parties, is sort of playing a spoiler role. Otherwise, for the time being, most of the players are in this collective game.

I would say it is more likely than not that there will be a new President elected, you know, 51–49. Hard to say.

The second most likely would simply be that the post will fall vacant for a while or a long time.

The third possibility would be the extension of the term of the current President. That is very difficult, very unlikely. That requires a two-thirds consensus. That does not exist.

So either we elect a new President or we fall into a period of a vacancy.

The key factor that created this momentum and the key factor that could ruin this momentum is the regional environment. I think we happen to be at a moment, even though Geneva did not succeed, it did happen, and we have moved from sides expecting that the other side is going to fall within 2 months to a realization that this is going on for a long time. There has been sort of a moment of a diplomacy. How long that will last in the region—weeks, months—if in that sort of honeymoon period we can go ahead and elect a President, we will be lucky. If we miss that, I think we will go back to what we had before, which is paralysis. We could not have elections for Parliament. We could not form a government, and we could not elect a President.

Senator KAINE. Mr. Nerguizian.

Mr. NERGUIZIAN. Mr. Chairman, most of the factions in Lebanon have been competing, whether it is domestically or in Syria, with an assumption that somehow the crisis would be resolved within a relatively fixed or short period. I think it has dawned on every faction that matters that Syria's civil war is in every way going to be a decade of long-term pressures and dynamics that they, whether they like it or not, are going to have to cooperate with each other on in terms of the next steps. So you have right now a Cabinet. Beyond the formation of this Cabinet and its ministerial statement, you have a number of other institutions that are deeply dependent on this. For example, in the LAF, you have an organization that is known as the Military Council, which has traditionally played the role of a buffer dealing with a lot of the sectarian pressures. It remains largely vacant. You have the longer term issue of who will be the next LAF commander. And all of these events, filling key leadership posts, dealing with the Presidency, and then dealing with leadership of the LAF in the long term—they all require a set of factors that are like delicate sequencing.

But, frankly, Mr. Chairman, I think it is difficult to sit and think realistically about who the people are that could fill in these posts. The Presidency, just as Cabinet formation has shown us, is deeply precarious and uncertain. None of us can predict how this will play out. You have only a finite set of players that are being considered anecdotally.

But the bigger issue, I think—and I highlight this in my statement—is that you have a Christian community in Lebanon and frankly in the region that, for better or for worse, feels that it needs a strong President or at least a President that enjoys broad communal support. Now, will we get to that in the scenarios that Dr. Salem described, or will this map out in a way that is far more unstable? It is difficult to predict, and I frankly am careful about making those sorts of assumptions.

Senator KAINE. I asked the previous panel the question of whether in its internal politics in Lebanon, Hezbollah has been affected or seen any erosion of its political support because of the decision to go all in in the Syrian civil war. And I would like to hear each of you sort of address—the role of Hezbollah in Syria is one thing, but how has it affected their place in Lebanese society and sort of their political profile at the current time?

Dr. SALEM. Well, initially it was not a very popular move amongst Hezbollah's own supporters. Initially when the uprising in Syria seemed like part of the early Arab Spring, pro-democracy, the Assad regime was firing on people, there was not a clear understanding of why should Hezbollah get involved. There was not yet the appearance on the other side of these radical al-Qaeda-related groups. But Hezbollah's popularity in the community is so overwhelming on so many levels. There is no real contest there. But even if there was some reluctance, there was no real questioning of the decision, some complaining but no real questioning.

I would say that the community certainly is maybe drained, is very concerned, but I think they have been convinced to some degree that, indeed, there is a major Sunni radical threat to them. Now, whether that threat was partly created by what the Assad regime itself did and you get the enemy that you would desire, but indeed this threat has become real. It has become real to all Lebanese. It certainly has become real to the Shiite community in Lebanon. So I would say they are paying a very high price. They are not happy about it, but there is not any major questioning right now of the decision.

I think the major impact on Hezbollah is long-term, that this is effectively a force which was designed, A, to push back at Israeli occupation. Secondly, it was designed as a deterrent for Iran against any potential Israeli or American strike on Iran. That is its function. Now, since Syria left Lebanon, they have had to be the policeman in Lebanon. So they have turned into internal politics. Now they have to be the policeman and the army in Syria. They are so overreaching, so overextended. In the long term, this is something that drains them, drains the community, makes them long-term very vulnerable, similar to what the PLO experienced between 1975 and eventually 1982.

What I sort of worry about most is that the border region between Lebanon and Syria and Israel, which has been stable for the last 8 years, in the long term will likely not be because the powers are shifting. And Hezbollah is not in a good position. It is fighting on many fronts. It was not designed to do so. The community is too small to sustain it.

Senator KAINE. Mr. Nerguizian.

Mr. NERGUIZIAN. Mr. Chairman, Hezbollah always knew that taking this level of action in Syria would cost it support within the broader Lebanese Sunni community, to say nothing of broader Arab popular support. That has essentially come to pass. They no longer enjoy that broad range of backing at the regional level. But that is the cost, as Hezbollah sees it, of creating that strategic depth that it thinks it needs.

The other side of this is that on net balance, Hezbollah's role has brought some degree of predictability, perhaps not in the way that many would like, along the Lebanese-Syrian frontier. If one were to ask 4 or 5 years ago would Hezbollah allow or sanction or facilitate the establishment of better border relations, more demarcation, a robust security regime along the border, one would be hesitant to say, yes. But the dynamics are such now that you have at least an opportunity to do good, to do good in terms of the Lebanese and institutions like the LAF focusing on building up these institutions and structures along the border.

You also have all the patterns that Dr. Salem described in terms of what the long-term radicalization and instability effects are. In every way that matters, radicalization within the Sunni community in Lebanon and the inflow of fighters presents as much of a threat to mainstream Sunnis in the country as it does to mainstream Shiites. And that has bought Hezbollah some breathing room.

But in the long term, I think there is no doubt. You have a transformation that is taking place that is part of internal Shiite dynamics but also part of a broader regional pattern that includes Saudi Arabia, Iran, and the United States. Right now, it is not clear, if there is a resolution of the Syria conflict, what will be Hezbollah's future, but what is broadly clear to me is that Iran is looking for a posteriori arrangement. And by that, what I mean is if there is going to be some kind of a new regional order that ties in negotiations on the nuclear file and that ties in on the U.N. Blue Line and Hezbollah, it is something that they would like to see occur as a result of an arrangement or a framework, not before. So you are going to continue to see continued support by Iran.

And within the Shiite community, I have to agree there is no real basis to say that there is anything more than marginal dissent within the community. Hezbollah has been very effective, and frankly, their opponents have helped as well to create a narrative of self-defense and countering terrorism, which has become in many ways a national reality.

Senator KAINE. Thank you.

Dr. SALEM. Mr. Chairman?

Senator KAINE. Yes, please.

Dr. SALEM. I just want to add something that is sort of relevant about the refugee situation and security, both Hezbollah and national security.

You have a million, maybe up to a million and a half, refugees from Syria. The vast majority are Sunnis. Lebanon, in the sense by what is happening Syria by Hezbollah's actions, is effectively turning into a Sunni majority country, and yet Hezbollah is fighting in Syria and Lebanon and putting itself in a very precarious situation. The country has absorbed a quarter of the number of its population in refugees, and yet, ''nothing has happened.'' And one marvels at that.

The metaphor I sort of use is it is like you are pouring fuel into the basement. Nothing has happened yet, but it takes one match for that to explode. The experience of Lebanon or other communities with refugees, whether it was the Palestinians—it took several years. But if and when that refugee population becomes mobilized and militarized, as some groups in Syria and the region are trying to do, once that happens, then that fuel ignites and neither Hezbollah nor Lebanon can control it.

For us that means and maybe for U.S. policy, yes, it has been survivable so far but, A, we need to stem the flow and, B, we need to find ways to get those people starting to go back either in a resolved Syria or safe havens, you know, get the flow reversed. Lebanon—I mean, one marvels that it has survived so far, but this could detonate at any point in the near future and it requires urgent attention to be reversed, not just treated symptomatically.

Senator KAINE. Dr. Salem, your comments really echo Mr. Silverman on the earlier panel when he said we are just sort of in uncharted territory. Twenty-five percent of the population equivalent being as refugees. So far, no massive match strike, but we just do not know when that point would come in terms of that breaking point that you testified to.

In terms of the magnitude of the refugee challenge, moving to that, Mr. Nerguizian made the point of everyone probably thought that this civil war would be something that would be resolved sooner, and everybody is kind of waking up to a reality that it is not going to be a quick resolution. It is going to take significant time.

Do you think Lebanese civil society, the NGO community, the International Support Group—are they appropriately now changing their thinking and planning to treat this not as an emergency situation, but really to start to look at it as a long-term problem, in which case the way you manage it is going to be different than kind of a traditional emergency relief operation? For either of you.

Mr. NERGUIZIAN. Mr. Chairman, one of the side effects of regularly traveling to Lebanon—and I traveled in 2013 about six times—is that you get to see the gradual evolution of all the patterns you just described. You no longer have any of the optimism that you can have short-term efforts with a quick payoff. All the realities now, whether it is the NGO community, the humanitarian aid structures that are operating in Lebanon, or emerging structures like the International Support Group, are all going to have to exercise a great degree of strategic patience in all of this.

This is not a civil war that is just born out of protests over a short-term period as a result of droughts. It is the basic collapse of a state structure that has been kind of limping along since as far back as the Second World War. You are looking at a transformational moment. And whether it is the ISG or local forces, I am seeing a gradual, slow, and difficult shift to this.

But it has always been a key challenge in terms of resourcing. You have all of the impacts, not unlike those we have seen here in the United States tied to national resourcing and aid that are now coming to bear. You do not have the kinds of funds that are required readily available. And the countries that do have them are mainly in the gulf and have interests that are not necessarily tied to finding a quick and stabilizing effect on Lebanon and may be too closely linked to their own strategic imperatives in terms of regional competition.

But that is where I think U.S. and allied influence is critical. It plays a key role in shaping the choices of some of these countries that do also depend on the United States—for example, in the case of the gulf security architecture. The United States can play a positive role in shaping some of this because I think that there is an acceptance, at least within the U.S. interagency, not to say at the broader national level and the policy community, that this is a decade of instability.

Senator KAINE. Dr. Salem.

Dr. SALEM. Well, I mean, I would emphasize—I mean, I agree with all of that, and one must prepare for that. But I also definitely think that the world and the region cannot afford for this to go on for a decade. The regime in Syria has proven willing to fight to the last Syrian, to destroy all of Syria. It is willing to maintain power over part of a devastated Syria rather than share power with others over a united Syria. It is a regime that only understands force. When force was threatened against it, within days it made a major concession.

So from a policy perspective, it is such a dire crisis that it needs a much more robust interdiction. And I know this is a debate that has been going on in other chambers and so on. But looking at Lebanon, Jordan, Turkey, Iraq, the whole region, Iranian gulf tensions, tensions among U.S. allies in the gulf themselves, which have complicated the situation in Syria and in Iraq and elsewhere, yes, the United States wants to disengage, but the United States is still the biggest player in the region. Both allies and opponents look to it to figure out their own policy. This conflict—one cannot afford to leave it go on and on.

Now, what that means, what difficult decisions must be taken I do not know. I for one know that Lebanon cannot survive 2 more years, 3 more years of this. As we said, we are in uncharted territory. Although we have been in similar situations before with large refugee populations, it meant the destruction of Lebanon and 16 years of civil war in Lebanon. So we cannot at all be complacent. We can be thankful that we survived these 3 years.

But the lesson I take away is, yes, maybe prepare for the worst, but what needs to be done is again redoubled efforts to end this conflict. And I think in 2013 and 2014, there was a major initiative from the United States on the chemical weapons thing. It got immediate results. There was a great effort from Secretary Kerry which got at least some progress on the diplomatic front. This is not completely hopeless, but it requires more heavy lifting. And it needs to end. It cannot go on for years and years.

Senator KAINE. I very much share that view. While we are disappointed, obviously, with the path of the Geneva discussions in Syria, there is no substitute for those discussions, and even if the opportunity or the hope is just a flicker, we have got to do what we can to keep that ember alive.

It is the case the United States is the largest provider of humanitarian support for Syrian refugees outside the country. We are working on dismantling one of largest chemical weapons stockpiles in the world. That has been a significant diplomatic project. And while there have been aspects of the progress of that destruction that we are not happy with, we are, nevertheless, pursuing it and going forward, and we will untill its completion.

The challenge about the delivery of humanitarian aid is a significant one right now, but we were at least gratified that Russia dropped its veto posture in the Security Council over the delivery of humanitarian aid within Syria. If we could do that in a more aggressive way, that might stanch the flow of additional refugees out. It might. But the test of that Security Council resolution is obviously going to be pretty apparent, pretty quickly, to see whether actually we are able to do that delivery of aid or not. Much more heavy lifting has to be done. The engagement is there. The results have not been what we want but that does not mean that we need to back off.

I asked the previous panel—and, Mr. Nerguizian, I think you addressed this briefly in your testimony. Talk to us about the Lebanese Armed Forces in this inclusion aspect. To a first-time visitor, on the political side this delicate balance between the March 8/March 14 and others, the Sunni-Shia, Christian, the way this is balanced is very delicate. And when you cannot find that delicate balance, you end up with a caretaker Prime Minister. You end up with a government that cannot form. As we had brief interactions in this visit with the Lebanese Armed Forces, it seemed like it was less a group here of Sunnis, a group here of Shias, a group here of Christians, but a more integrated and inclusive armed forces. But that was from a brief visit. And I would be curious as to both of your sense on, is the Lebanese Armed Forces inclusive in that way, and is that inclusion within an armed forces of 60,000-plus people—does that offer lessons that can be helpful lessons more broadly in Lebanese civil society?

Mr. NERGUIZIAN. Well, Mr. Chairman, it is first critical to point out that the LAF reflects the socioeconomics and demographics of the time. I do not want to get into too much detail because I could easily write a book on the issue.

But if you were to look at the LAF in 1965, you would see an overwhelming number of Shiites because the LAF then, as now, was a vehicle for socioeconomic advancement. It was a chance for communities or demographics to uplift themselves.

When you fast forward to 2014, what you see is a pattern where the overwhelming majority of the LAF in terms of manpower is now Sunni. And when I say "overwhelming," I mean 42 percent. This reflects the reality of a force that is recruiting heavily from the north and heavily from Aakkar because these are provinces that frankly need the income and need the structure. You have a pension plan with benefits and the promise that eventually your children might not have to deal with either military service, or move on to other strata in the economy.

But beyond this, which does exist, you do have to bear in mind the officer corps, unlike the demographics of the broader force, is very heavily regulated in terms of which sect is represented and how. You have broadly a 50–50 split in terms of the officer corps of some 3,500 personnel. You do not have any quotas within the broader force. And this trickles up all the way to the top in terms of deputy chiefs of staff, chief of staff, the army commander, and so on.

And I think what does give this force a positive esprit de corps, to use the analogy, as opposed to one that is divisive is that over the history of the LAF going back to 1943, you have had an effort to incubate an idea, an idea that this is not a nonsectarian Lebanon or a nonsectarian LAF, but rather that this is a cross-sectarian country, and this is an institution that has to represent those interests.

Beyond that, you have a nucleus of officers, many of which are now at the command level, who were trained in 1980, 1981, and 1982. This is in many ways the vintage generation of LAF officers and they now are at their prime. They are cross-sectarian. They come from all the communities, and they genuinely want to do good. And if they are to advance professionally and to move on in their careers and play a role in the next 2 or 3 years, that is favorable not just for Lebanon. It is favorable for regional stability. If that opportunity is missed, you are looking at the next generational gap, somewhere between 10 and 15 years within which you have to wait for the next crop of officers to mature and play a role. And these demographics are delicate and difficult and dense. I am happy to go into greater detail after the testimony.

Senator KAINE. Yes, that is helpful.

Dr. Salem.

Dr. SALEM. Yes, I would agree with that. I mean, indeed, in a sense everybody's cousin is in the army. Everybody is serving the army as a family, and that is extremely important for national identity and people's general respect for the army. Now, there have been incidents here and there where there have been remarks about this thing or that thing, but it is one of the major institutions which reinforces Lebanese identity and attachment to the state.

It is also important to note, though, that this army, being a multisectarian or cross-sectarian army, reflects the very society it is part of. It cannot be used as a blunt instrument internally against any community. Many people ask why does it not fight Hezbollah or fight—you know. It cannot engage directly in any internal conflict. It can maintain peace. It can create stability. It can protect borders. It plays a very important role in reinforcing basic political understandings and political accommodations. So it has it strengths. It also has its limitations. It has done reasonably well in this period.

But the Lebanese political system also, for all of its faults and dysfunctions, is a fairly ingenious and inclusive one and makes sure that all the communities feel they have a stake, that they are not threatened by the state or any decisions taken in that state. There might be lessons there for Syria of 2025 or even Iraq, which is having a very difficult time managing a multicommunal reality.

Senator KAINE. So I am going to ask you to make a general choice. For future U.S. military assistance to the Lebanese Armed Forces, what is more important? Training assistance or equipment and weaponry?

Mr. NERGUIZIAN. Mr. Chairman, the net effect of U.S. training has been to elevate the special forces to being true special forces by regional standards. They are not just units in name alone.

What you have now, though, is an urgent need to stand up the rest of the force. The core 3,700 SOF personnel, special forces personnel, continue to benefit from this training and not just from the United States But you also have 11 mechanized brigades and 5 intervention regiments that, frankly, are going to be at the forefront of what is going to be an even more difficult and challenging period for the LAF. You have a force that is also gradually swinging south from the northern border with Syria down past the Bekaa frontier, and it will eventually, through the deployment of the second border regiment, encircle parts of Lebanon where you have communities that, frankly, are not quite sure what the intentions of the LAF are.

Now, in parallel to their efforts to manage this—and the LAF does want to essentially have a soft glove approach of partnership and working in partnership with communities like the one in Arsal, and that is a key point.

I think the United States has a key role to play in standing up the third and fourth border regiments. This is not to say that we can pick equipment over training. Frankly, one is nothing without the other, as you know.

Senator KAINE. Right.

Mr. NERGUIZIAN. But right now, one has to always revert back and look at what the CDP, the capabilities development plan, says. The overarching tenets there are not just about acquisition and systems. The LAF has learned a lot about that. It is far more focused on building an LAF 2025 dealing with all of the pressures Dr. Salem and myself described. So I think while we have to prioritize some aspects of training, it is always going to be a case-by-case analysis in terms of looking whether or not to prioritize that over land systems, naval systems, or other combat mechanisms.

Senator KAINE. Dr. Salem.

Dr. SALEM. Aram is the expert on this. So I defer to him.

Senator KAINE. I just report to you the opinion of the U.S. military leadership in Lebanon about the professionalism of the special forces is just as you suggest, Mr. Nerguizian. They were highly complimentary of the professionalism of the special forces. As you mentioned, it is not special forces in name only. It is special forces that they have merited by their training and their performance.

And I was struck in meeting with Lebanon Armed Forces leadership how many of them talked about their training either in Lebanon with United States military forces or here in the United States. Some of the training that we do of foreign military leaders here in the United States or in-country are so cost-effective compared to other things that we do. I am on the Budget Committee too, and we are wrestling with all these budgetary issues.

After we were in Lebanon, we went to Egypt and I had a lengthy meeting with General el-Sisi. We have a lot of challenges right now in that relationship because of some of the suspensions of aid that we have put in place after the events of June and July 2013. But over all of those challenges that we have, the year that General el-Sisi spent at the National War College in 2006 in Carlisle, PA, gives him a real understanding of the United States and a real affection for that military-to-military relationship. And in a period where there are some disagreements and challenges, having a background of ''but we trained together, I know these people and they know me, we got a problem, but we ought to be able to work for it,'' that year of training or the training that we provide to leaders in the LAF—I think the value of it is so much greater than the incremental cost of training one more person at the War College or doing a little bit more training in Lebanon. So I am a strong supporter of this kind of training going forward.

Let me ask you this. How about the question about the effect of a rapprochement with appropriate skepticism, some increasing rapprochement with Iran? The interim joint plan of agreement around the nuclear negotiation then has led to a larger discussion about trying to find a diplomatic resolution of this issue of Iran's nuclear weapons program. It is focused on their nuclear weapons program. It is not focused on other issues. But in human experience, we understand that finding an agreement on one aspect makes it easier potentially to find an agreement on another. If there was some rapprochement between the West and Iran or maybe between Saudi Arabia and Iran, would the likely effect of that on the internal political dynamic in Lebanon be positive or would it be hard to predict what that effect would be?

Dr. SALEM. Well, if I may, I mean, there has been a perceived rapprochement or at least dialogue between the United States and Iran, as there has been between the United States and Syria over the chemical weapons deal. And many in the region, particularly the Gulf States who 2 years ago thought that the Assad regime's days were numbered, that the United States and Western position was clear, and also thought that the United States and others had a very firm position isolating, containing, or even combating Iran— now they wake up to a very different world in which Assad is sort of a partner in the long-term chemical weapons deal where he can drag his feet pretty much for a very long time. Iran is in negotiations, which might take a very long time and which certainly at least indicate that the United States is coexisting with Iran and with the Assad regime for the current future.

Now, what did that create in terms of dynamics? I think it created several. First of all, it created panic in some countries in the region, in the gulf, and some degree Turkey. For a while, that caused them to escalate and want to go their own way. But I think in the last few months, I think we have seen a more sober reaction that, well, this is the new reality. You know, this is going to take some time. Expectation that Assad is going to fall tomorrow is not real. The United States is not about to do it and is not as tough against Iran as it was. And that is what I referred to that we are living through now, a moment particularly from Saudi Arabia, to some degree from Turkey and the Emirates and Kuwait, a sense of movement a bit toward accommodation, some stabilization for now in this particular phase.

But I think what is missing from this entire picture is that the United States is negotiating with Iran over the nuclear file, but from the Iranian perspective and from the states in the region, Iran is maintaining and indeed extending its hegemony in Iraq and in Syria and in Lebanon. And the two ships are sort of linked. The more they talk with the United States, the more they have the free hand, they feel, either in the Assad regime bombing civilians or Iran supporting whether it is Maliki, Assad, Hezbollah, and so on. And that creates more conflict and more tension.

Now this, obviously, is all complicated and, as you said, requires heavy lifting. But the region is sort of in a conflict system and the United States is only dealing with parts of it and often creating repose somewhere and tension somewhere else.

What is certainly missing is the United States engaging Iran with the states of the region to talk about things beyond the nuclear issue, which is Iran's projection of power into Iraq, Syria, and Lebanon and doing so in a very flagrant way that breaks all norms of international relations and so on. If the Middle East is to see any kind of stability, that cannot continue. And unfortunately, that is not part of the Iranian-United States discussions. So I think if it remains at that level, indeed it could be destabilizing.

Senator KAINE. One sentiment I picked up on in my travels in the region that it was actually very helpful to kind of hear this expression was the anxiety in the region not about the failure of the United States-Iran negotiation over the nuclear program, but there is an anxiety about its success. If there was success, would the United States say, okay, our work is done here? We have reached a deal on the nuclear program and we do not need to worry about these other issues of projection of Iranian power in the region and how that could destabilize regimes. There seems to be some significant concern that the United States would feel good about a deal on the nuclear program and then potentially say we do not need to worry about the other issues when, for many of the nations in the region, they are equally or more concerned about the projection of power and the destabilizing effects of Iranian policy, as they are about the nuclear program. So it was helpful to hear some of those dynamics when we were there. And that sounds like one of your cautionary warnings to us.

Mr. Nerguizian.

Mr. NERGUIZIAN. Mr. Chairman, the three issues that frankly cannot be disassociated from each other are how the gulf and Iran are competing in the Levant, the P5+1 talks you described, but also I think the core issue that countries in the gulf are fundamentally misinterpreting or getting the wrong message about what, if anything, is the Rebalance to Asia. The interpretation in the gulf is that the United States is abandoning the gulf security architecture. And frankly, every meeting that we have conducted in the region reinforces this view. I think it is incumbent on the administration and frankly the broader diplomatic community to just make it clear. There is no pivot to Asia. You have an acceptance and an understanding by key NATO allies that Iran's conventional and asymmetric forces are squarely focused on the gulf, and that drives a great deal of this whether it is competing in Iraq or competing in Syria.

But in all of this, I think again key countries have underestimated just how severe the scales are in terms of what Syria is doing. You have a new generation of fighters returning home to countries in the gulf, returning to Europe. You have all of the patterns of the Arab uprising in terms of broad socioeconomics, labor markets, which we did not discuss in detail but that drive a lot of this. And I think even countries like Iran and Saudi Arabia that look at what is happening in Syria as zero sum, in terms of who wins or loses, are slowly coming around to a view that I think the United States has slowly moved to, which is that you need a pragmatic response to a broader trend. I agree with Dr. Salem. There need to be short-term solutions, but this is a long pattern. The arc of history will be long in the region in terms of what the end state will look like. You need metrics of stability. And if linking what is happening in Syria and as a result in Lebanon to P5+1, in concert with a successful strategic communications effort from the gulf, produces more stability, then so be it.

Senator KAINE. Dr. Salem, I have one last question for you. You indicated in your testimony—you talked a little bit about the economic issues that could be positive in Lebanon if there is a pursuit of natural gas development. And you said I could say a word more about that if you were interested. I actually am sort of interested in your expertise on these economic issues. What do you see as sort of the opportunities that these gas reserves provide for the Lebanese economy and the likelihood that those opportunities will be accessed and taken advantage of in the near or medium term?

Dr. SALEM. Yes, I have worked a lot on this and met with the people and companies that are involved. This is a very interesting and somewhat complicated situation.

The reserves—of course, they are not proven. One has to drill and so on. But from even the estimates of many of the companies or their expectations, there are very, very serious, particularly the gas reserves. They are a bit deep. So they are expensive to get at. Much will depend on at that time what are the market outlets and what is the money calculations behind it.

But I see it really in two stages. Stage one is going ahead with the bidding to which many of the major oil companies of the West and the East have applied to bid, and the bid round was supposed to happen last year because the government still needed to issue a few decrees. When it resigned, it was a caretaker government and could not go forward. The first stage is going ahead with the bidding round, and for the first 4 to 5 to 6 years, there will be no revenue. You know, maybe within 5–6 years, you begin to drill. You begin to get some energy, but to turn that into money, it might be a 7–10 years window.

But what is important about phase one, if you have major oil players from the United States and Russia and Europe and China engaged in this sector in the eastern Mediterranean, alongside Israel and Cyprus, which relates to then Turkey and the EU and all of that, it might create for Lebanon an investment in its stability and its long-term viability because of the importance of energy, similar to how the gulf sort of gets its stability and security. The gulf countries are a strange—you know, tribes and this, but they survive because they have important resources. Other parts of the world sometimes have that as well. That is very important for Lebanon's geostrategic environment if the East and West agree that this must be a peaceful zone because there are important resources here.

Now, actually moving forward on what is the economic value of this, the first thing is to figure out how to get it to market. The market is effectively Europe. The original approach was or the plan was certainly to take it overland to Turkey which would mean through Syria. As long as the war there is raging, you cannot do that, but that is the most cost-effective way. And I would indicate that part of the war for Syria has to do with who is going to control the future of eastern Mediterranean energy.

The other way to do it, which Israel is exploring, is whether to do it through LNG in Cyprus and put it on ships or possibly from Cyprus an undersea pipeline to Turkey and then Turkey gets it to market. So it gets into a lot of geopolitics and relations.

If Lebanon can get this to market and sell it, that would be— well, let me say two things. The energy itself, the gas—if it is extracted, the first use of it is directly into the Lebanese electricity production, which would take the biggest bill from Lebanon's public finances off the records as what we pay to create electricity. That would be the first and most direct easing for the Lebanese public finances.

The second part is if we begin to sell on the markets. The money, according to the law that was passed, will be put into a sovereign wealth fund. The law for the sovereign wealth fund and the details of how that money will be spent has not yet been negotiated, but the principle of creating a sovereign wealth fund, which is the proper approach in principle, has been made law and a future parliament will have to pass a law as to what the wealth fund will use the money for. Will it be to draw down debt? Will be capital investment? Or will it be just insurance for the future? The Norwegians are working very closely with the Lebanese. They have the best model. There are other models as well.

So it is geostrategic stability first and within a decade, if they move ahead, beginning to move ahead on some economic benefits which would be very significant.

During that whole period, there would be a benefit that companies both upstream, downstream will begin setting up in Lebanon to prepare for this sector, and that in itself creates economic activity in Lebanon which creates jobs and growth, all of this overshadowed by the war in Syria. So it is pretty tough going. But still, there is serious interest in the international community, even with the war going on, for the bids to go forward.

Most of the gas and so on is not in the border area. There are fields. It is not exactly clear because one has to drill to be sure. It is likely that one of the main Israeli fields maybe dips up a bit into southern—the very disputed zone. But it is really not a major issue in the sense that there is 90 percent of drilling that can take place that has nothing to do with the Israeli border issues. So we can go on for 20–30 years without even touching that issue. If people want to avoid it, it is definitely avoidable. The challenges are to get ahead with the bidding round, to begin the process, to find ways to get it eventually to market and to have some security and stability over this decade.

Senator KAINE. I want to thank you both for being here and for your testimony. One of the challenges of being a junior Senator is I am usually at hearings where I get to ask questions for 5 minutes. The ability to have two panels and have 2 hours where I can ask all the questions I want is a great satisfaction to the policy glutton in me.

Your expertise is very much appreciated. This is a very important relationship. And I frankly worry that in the story of Syria, the effect in Jordan has been a little better known, as it should be. It should be well known. The effect in Turkey has been a little better known, as it should be. It is important that the effect in Lebanon is very well known here in Congress and in this country. You have helped with that today. I look forward to continuing to work together with you.

And with that, the hearing is adjourned.

[Whereupon, at 5:37 p.m., the hearing was adjourned.]